EDITORIAL RESEARCH REPORTS
ON

THE
U.S. ECONOMY
UNDER
STRESS

Timely Reports to Keep
Journalists, Scholars and the Public
Abreast of Issues, Events and Trends

Published by Congressional Quarterly, Inc.
1414 22nd Street, N.W.
Washington, D.C. 20037

About the Cover

*The cover was designed by staff artist Richard Pottern.
Art Director Howard Chapman.*

Published in September 1975

Library of Congress Catalogue Card Number 75-18999
International Standard Book Number 0-87187-082-7

Editorial Research Reports
Editor Emeritus, Richard M. Boeckel
Editor, Hoyt Gimlin

Contents

FOREWORD

As these words are being written in the late summer of 1975, the American economy appears to be emerging from the worst recession since the Thirties. Signs of recovery are breaking through yesterday's forecasts of impending doom. The good news, however tentative, is reason for thanksgiving but, as yet, not congratulations. Although the country has endured the strains of inflation and recession with a minimum of visible social dislocation, the U.S. economy remains under stress.

Unemployment is receding only slowly—President Ford predicts that it may not fall below 6 per cent during the remainder of this decade. A college degree no longer assures a job. Inflation has drained away a sizable share of the American family's buying power and severely eroded the life savings of the aged. The nation's biggest city has had to be bailed out, and other cities throughout the country face the prospect of going broke. A number of leading thinkers believe that a continued slowdown in economic growth will threaten the quality of American life.

This book comprises nine separate reports written since December examining specific segments of the economy. The first three reports form a section whose perspective is largely that of the individual's concern—unemployment and underemployment, retirement security and consumer credit. The second section appraises the woes of three major business sectors—railroads, utilities and publishing. The third section maps out the government's response through fiscal control, revenue sharing and antitrust action. Together, these reports portray an economy under stress.

Hoyt Gimlin
Editor

September 1975
Washington, D.C.

PART 1
Impact on People

Underemployment in America

by

Mary Costello

**1 9 7 5
July 11**

UNDEREMPLOYMENT IN AMERICA

UNEMPLOYMENT has captured the national spotlight in recent months but, with a new crop of graduates in the labor force, a related problem is now receiving attention. This is the problem of underemployment—working at a job that does not make good use of one's ability, training or experience. Unlike unemployment, whose figures are compiled nationally each month by the U.S. Bureau of Labor Statistics (BLS), there is no official or objective measurement of underemployment. But its prevalence is well known. A study of working conditions conducted for the Department of Labor in 1974 found that 35 per cent of all American workers believed they were overqualified for their jobs.[1] Myron Clark, former president of the Society for the Advancement of Management, puts the figure at about 80 per cent.

As the demand for jobs, particularly professional jobs, continues to exceed the supply, the number of highly qualified persons working part-time at low wages continues to increase. According to BLS figures, the number of "subemployed" workers who wanted full-time jobs rose from 2.5 million in late 1973 to about 4 million in the spring of 1975. Employees at several companies are accepting pay cuts and reductions in the number of working hours to prevent large-scale layoffs.

Instead of moving on to better jobs, as they might have expected to do a few years ago, many workers are being forced to remain where they are. *U.S. News & World Report* has noted that "alongside millions of jobless workers, a new category of recession victims is appearing—men and women locked into jobs they would rather forsake for something better. Their career goals temporarily flattened under the weight of spreading unemployment, these 'immobilized workers' are holding onto whatever jobs they have until the unemployment climate brightens."[2]

There is another opinion that economic recovery will not cure or even significantly reduce underemployment. James O'Toole of the Center for Futures Research at the University of

---

[1] Robert Quinn, "1972-73 Quality of Employment Survey," University of Michigan Survey Research Center.
[2] *U.S. News & World Report*, April 14, 1975.

3

Southern California, for one, feels that the problems of underemployment "are basic and enduring shortcomings in the labor market and will not vanish with the current recession."[3] O'Toole's thesis is a gloomy one. It holds that throughout the industrial world there are too many educated men and women and too few good jobs suitable for their training and skills. As a result, many young people who grew up believing that education was the key to career success will be forced to take unchallenging jobs in which they have little interest and where the opportunities for advancement are slight. In the process, many of the less-educated workers will be displaced.

Bleak Employment Outlook for College Graduates

O'Toole is not the only Cassandra. The Bureau of Labor Statistics, in a recent survey of the job outlook through 1985, found that "problems for college graduates will more likely be employment below the level of skill for which they were trained, resulting in job dissatisfaction and high occupational mobility rather than unemployment." According to the bureau's projections, there will be 800,000 more college graduates in the labor force by 1985 than there will be new job openings for them—15.3 million graduates between 1972 and 1985 and 14.5 million jobs.[4]

While long-range predictions are by their nature subject to change, two recent studies found that college graduates in virtually all fields were having difficulty finding jobs today. The June 18 issue of Northwestern University's *Endicott Report* revealed that business demand for graduates with bachelor's degrees had declined by 31 per cent since the organization's November 1974 survey. Opportunities for holders of postgraduate master's degrees were down by 18 per cent. The findings, based on questionnaires sent to more than 100 of the nation's largest corporations, applied to engineering, accounting and business administration graduates as well as to those in the liberal arts.

A survey in May 1975 by the College Placement Council in Bethlehem, Pa., also indicated that demand for graduates was down this year. In November, employers in business, industry, government and non-profit and educational institutions—excluding teachers—had indicated to the council that they would be hiring about 4 per cent fewer college graduates in 1975 than in 1974. But by May the estimate was for an 18 per cent drop.

The occupations surveyed were (1) engineering, (2) sciences, math and other technical fields, (3) business, and (4) non-

---

[3] "Planning for Total Employment," *The Annals* of the American Academy of Political and Social Science, March 1975, pp. 73-74.
[4] "Occupational Manpower and Training Needs," 1974, p. 27.

Department of Labor
projections, 1972-85:

15.3 million college graduates
14.5 million jobs

technical or liberal arts specialties. "No categories escaped the downturn," the council reported. Engineering, after three successive years of increased hiring, fell 20 per cent. The least affected category was sciences, math and other technical fields, which dropped 7 per cent at the bachelor's degree level. Business declined 28 per cent. Job openings for liberal arts graduates fell 9 per cent "on top of a 45 per cent decrease in 1970-71 and almost no subsequent improvement in the intervening years."

Judging from their comments, the study reported, "employers do not expect appreciable improvement in hiring until possibly next spring." This time lag poses difficulties for recent graduates. Paul E. Steiger reported in *The Los Angeles Times* on June 1 that "a recurring nightmare" for some 1975 graduates is their fear that it will be five or six years before economic conditions will improve enough so that companies will be hiring in large numbers again. And by that time, he quoted Northwestern University graduate Greg Daugherty as saying, "instead of hiring those of us who have fried hamburgers and delivered mail for five years, waiting for things to get better, companies will recruit fresh college graduates."

Far more than their predecessors, today's college students are faced with the problem of finding a marketable specialty. A decade ago, they were encouraged to prepare for careers in medicine, law, engineering, science and teaching, and assured they would find good jobs in those fields. Subsequently nearly all of those fields became surfeited with graduates. Today the American Medical Association, concerned about an oversupply of doctors, is demanding that the influx of foreign physicians be halted. There are now about 30,000 law degrees awarded each year. But the Department of Labor estimates that there will be openings for only 16,500 lawyers a year during the 1970s.

Economic problems in the late 1960s and early 1970s brought about a large-scale retrenchment in engineering. The number of students choosing this field dropped sharply and by 1973 there was a shortage of engineers. The shortage soon turned into another surplus. The National Science Foundation projects that by 1985 more than 20 per cent of those holding doctoral degrees in engineering and science will be employed in areas unrelated to their specialty, compared to less than 10 per cent in 1972. And Professor Allan N. Cartter of the University of California at Los Angeles, one of the first to warn about a surplus of college teachers, now believes that less than 10 per cent of the new Ph.D.s will find teaching jobs in academe in the next few years.

The BLS predicts that there will be job openings for architects, geophysicists, computer specialists, chemists, accountants, employment counselors and health-related paraprofessionals in the next decade. These predictions are based on the assumption that the number of men and women choosing careers in these fields will remain relatively stable. But if past trends are any indication, it is likely that students will flock to these professions and that the job demand will soon outpace the supply. Thus the very forecasts tend to become self-defeating.

Entrapment Feelings in Secondary Labor Market

The oversupply of college graduates has an impact on the whole work force. As educated young people wait in line for jobs, workers already in the labor force are aware that employers would have little difficulty replacing them and thus they remain on jobs which, in another era, they would probably have left for more satisfying work. As opportunities for advancement and career mobility in many fields lessen, these workers are often left with a feeling of entrapment. The Bureau of Labor Statistics, in its 1974-75 "Occupational Outlook for College Graduates," said: "In the future, workers without college degrees will probably have fewer opportunities to advance to professional positions.... Thus, while college graduates may face competition for jobs, those without a college education will face even greater competition for the better jobs."

"Dual labor market" theorists see the economy divided into a primary high-wage sector and a secondary low-wage sector.[5] The two labor sectors are not precisely defined in terms of which jobs fall into what categories. While it can be assumed that the secondary sector is made up mostly of blue-collar workers, not all blue-collar workers are in the secondary sector. Skilled laborers in many fields receive high wages and numerous job opportunities. Studies have shown that the income gap between white and skilled blue-collar workers has narrowed considerably. This gap can be expected to narrow further as college graduates compete for scarce white-collar jobs.

"A basic fact about semi-skilled working-class life: it is on a flat level.... There is not too much point in working hard to get somewhere for there is no place to go."

Victor C. Gerkiss, *Technological Man* (1969)

Much that has been written about the work-related "blue-collar blues"[6] is directed primarily at unskilled or semi-skilled work. The feelings of apathy, dissatisfaction, discontent, entrapment and alienation ascribed to workers in relatively mundane jobs will surely become more pronounced if, as feared, college graduates are forced to accept employment that ignores their training and shatters their expectations. It has been shown that highly educated or intelligent workers in unchallenging and tedious jobs tend to be less productive and more accident-prone than their less gifted co-workers.

Women, blacks, the young and the old are overrepresented in unskilled occupations. William B. Werther Jr., an Arizona State University professor, describes the effect of their underemployment on job performance. "Even mature people in mundane jobs are likely to give less than optimal performance because the job

---

[5] See "Primary and Secondary Labor Markets: A Critique of the Dual Approach" by Michael L. Wachter in *Brookings Papers on Economic Activity*, No. 3, 1974, p. 639.
[6] See "Productivity and the New Work Ethic," *E.R.R.*, 1972 Vol. I, p. 293.

limitations are frustrating. This frustration must be relieved, and unexplained absences, horseplay or other irresponsible behavior are some of the ways that such frustrated feelings can be dissipated."[7]

Government Programs to Relieve Unemployment

Some see the solution to the problems of unemployment, sub-employment and underemployment as the creation of thousands of public-service jobs. There are two basic types of public employment to combat these problems. The first, exemplified by Depression programs like the Works Progress Administration (WPA), focuses primarily on income maintenance for persons without jobs or with very low-paying jobs. The second, typified by many of the social programs during the 1960s, seeks to train persons with employment handicaps for permanent work.

The two major job programs of the 1970s sought to combine these approaches. The Public Employment Program (PEP), established under the Emergency Employment Act of 1971, and the Comprehensive Employment and Training Act (CETA) of 1973 were enacted to provide income maintenance for the unemployed "while emphasizing preferential consideration for members of special target groups (veterans, minorities and the disadvantaged) according to their representation among the unemployed."[8] These programs are intended as temporary relief until the economy improves.

In December 1974, Congress authorized $2.5 billion for state and local governments to hire unemployed workers for community-service jobs in education, health and day care, sanitation and recreation. In March, President Ford asked Congress for $2 billion to extend the public-service program for another year and to create more than 750,000 summer jobs. The bill Congress approved called for $5.3 billion; the President vetoed it as too inflationary. In June, Congress passed and Ford signed legislation appropriating $473 million for 840,000 summer jobs.

Public-service employment is often praised as a way of deriving needed public benefits from tax expenditures. But it is also regarded as an expedient rather than a long-term solution. James O'Toole wrote: "What kinds of jobs are being created? Not leaf raking perhaps, but jobs not likely to motivate the new generation of qualified workers."[9] A similar questioning of current public-service programs came from A. Dale Tussing, professor of economics at Syracuse University. Writing in the

---

[7] "Part-Timers: Overlooked and Undervalued," *Business Horizons*, February 1975, pp. 14-15.
[8] See "Manpower Report of the President," April 1975, p. 4.
[9] "The Reserve Army of the Underemployed," Part I, *Change*, May 1975, p. 32.

February 1975 issue of *Intellect* magazine, he observed: "To provide, through subsidized employment or direct public-sector hiring, still another set of low-paying, short-duration, dead-end jobs would make little if any contribution to the new unemployment. Instead, it is essential that the jobs created be of a long-term variety, contain a substantial on-the-job learning component, lead to possible advancement...."

Role of Education and Government

F ORMAL EDUCATION was not always viewed as the key to career success. Such industrial titans as John D. Rockefeller, Henry Ford and Andrew Carnegie had little schooling. Horatio Alger characters achieved success through hard work, clean living, and non-academic resourcefulness. Many of today's unemployed, underemployed or subemployed might well envy the opportunities that a bygone era seemed to offer anyone with the native intelligence and will to seize them.

The vast majority of 19th and early 20th century Americans were neither highly educated nor Horatio Alger successes. The rapid industrialization that followed the Civil War brought about a seemingly unending need for unskilled labor to man the factories and shops. "The workers who helped build this industrial empire often labored under harsh and hazardous conditions, lived in firetrap tenements, suffered unemployment and, even when working, received near starvation wages."[10] Employee discontent with wages, working conditions, long hours and unexpected layoffs led to often violent strikes and demands for unionization.

Most of the industrial workers were unskilled and uneducated; many were recent immigrants. High school was principally a preparation for college. In 1870, for example, 80 per cent of all high school graduates went on to college. College, in turn, led to a degree in the liberal arts and careers in law, medicine, teaching, the arts and some businesses. College graduates rarely had difficulty finding jobs in their chosen fields.

Beginning with the adoption of compulsory school attendance laws in many states around 1880, high school enrollment increased enormously. And as high school became the terminal point in the education of many young people, public demand for

---

[10] Jonathan Grossman and Judson MacLaury, "The Creation of the Bureau of Labor Statistics," *Monthly Labor Review*, February 1975, p. 21.

practical, career-minded education grew. Early vocational training programs were conceived as an attempt to "infuse new vitality into old curricula, to rouse student interest, to promote more sensible occupational choices, to raise the educational level of the laboring classes and to elevate all occupations to a millennium of culture and refinement."[11]

Academicians tended to be critical of efforts to train students for particular jobs. John Dewey, the philosopher and educator, attacked vocational education as undemocratic. The idea that a liberal arts education is the best preparation for work is still stressed by a number of American educators today. Typical of this thinking, University of Chicago President Robert Maynard Hutchins remarked in 1944: "The thing to do with vocational education is to forget it.... The task of the educational system is not to train hands for industry, but to prepare enlightened citizens for our democracy and to enrich the life of the individual by giving him a sense of purpose which will illuminate not merely the 40 hours he works but the 72 he does not."

Federal Government as Employer of Last Resort

Beginning with the Morrill Act of 1862, the federal government showed an interest in improving the skills of the labor force to meet the demands of technologically advancing agriculture and industry. The act provided the states grants of land to endow, support and maintain colleges to teach agriculture and the practical arts "to promote the liberal and practical education of the industrial classes." But until the depression of the 1930s, government concern with unemployment was directed toward the problems of supplying employers with needed workers rather than assuring working men of a sufficiency of jobs.

Massive unemployment forcibly turned the federal government's attention to a national problem of what to do with an idled labor force of unprecedented dimensions. By July 1932, wages were 60 per cent of their 1929 level, industry was operating at half the volume of 1929 and average monthly unemployment was running at 12 million, more than a quarter of the labor force. Many of those still employed were put on a shorter work week with less pay.

President Roosevelt, upon taking office on March 4, 1933, made unemployment relief one of the first orders of business. Over the next few years, millions of workers were hired and billions of dollars were spent on a host of programs. These included the Public Works Administration (PWA), the Civil Works Administration (CWA), the Federal Emergency Relief Administration (FERA), the Civilian Conservation Corps (CCC), the

---

[11] Grant Vern, *Man, Education and Work* (1964), p. 49.

National Youth Administration (NYA) and the Works Progress Administration (WPA).[12]

The best known and most controversial of these job-making programs was the WPA, established as an independent agency in 1935. It was a massive hire-the-unemployed project with the primary purpose of getting individuals and families off relief and putting them to work on socially useful jobs. Workers included the skilled and unskilled, professional and blue-collar. Over the eight years of its existence, WPA spent almost $11 billion and employed 8.5 million persons. Projects ranged from renovating 85,000 public buildings and constructing 16,000 water and sewer systems to writing an acclaimed series of state guidebooks. But the program's emphasis on income maintenance made it a target for criticism as "leaf-raking make-work."

At the end of World War II, however, there was widespread support for federal programs aimed at avoiding a repetition of the unemployment dislocations of the 1930s. President Truman on Sept. 6, 1945, called for "a national reassertion of the right to work for every American citizen able and willing to work" and "a declaration of the ultimate duty of government to use its own resources if all other methods fail to prevent prolonged unemployment." The next year, after protracted debate, Congress passed the Employment Act of 1946 which declared that "it is the continuing policy and responsibility of the federal government to use all practicable means...to promote maximum employment, production and purchasing power."

But Washington did little to create jobs for the unemployed during the first three postwar recessions, in 1948, 1953 and 1957. The first significant legislation came after the 1960-61 recession when unemployment approached 7 per cent, the highest since the Depression. The Manpower Development and Training Act (Md-TA) of 1962, enacted to retrain workers with obsolete skills, put the government directly into job training. MDTA programs provided both on-the-job and institutional training for unemployed and underemployed adults and youth.

College Education Boom Following World War II

In the postwar recessions, unemployment and underemployment fell most heavily on the unskilled and undereducated. While these groups had always borne the major burden of employment dislocations, technological developments in the late 1940s and 1950s intensified the problem. As the demand for unskilled and semi-skilled workers waned, job opportunities for professional and other white-collar workers increased enormously.

---

[12] For background, see "Inflation and Job Security," *E.R.R.*, 1974 Vol. II, p. 707.

Ten Years of College Enrollments

Fall	Number of Students	Increase Over Prior Year
1974	10,321,539	6.5%
1973	9,694,297	4.3
1972	9,204,000	2.0
1971	9,025,031	4.3
1970	8,566,333	7.2
1969	7,978,408	5.4
1968	7,571,636	8.7
1967	6,963,687	8.2
1966	6,438,477	7.9
1965	5,967,411	12.2

SOURCE: U.S. Office of Education

Until the middle or late 1960s, the demand for skilled, educated workers seemed open-ended. Teachers, doctors, engineers, scientists, lawyers and other professionals generallly had a wide variety of jobs to choose from and ample opportunity to advance in their chosen careers. Education was almost universally accepted as the key to career mobility and the rising level of schooling for the population reflected this acceptance. In 1940, for example, only about 37 per cent of the workers aged 25-29 had graduated from high school; thirty years later, the figure had jumped to over 75 per cent. During that period, the percentage of 25-29 year olds with college or higher degrees rose from 5.8 per cent to 16.4 per cent.

The federal government encouraged the college boom. Under the Serviceman's Readjustment Act of 1944—the G.I. Bill—Washington provided veterans enrolled as full-time students a living allowance of from $75 to $120 a month and made direct payments to the institution for tuition, fees and other costs of up to $500 a month. Largely as a result of this program, male college enrollment jumped from 928,000 in 1945-46 to 1,659,249 in 1947-48.[13]

Congress reacted to the launching of the first Russian satellite, Sputnik I, in 1957 by passing the National Defense Education Act of 1958. That law provided scholarships, loans and grants to improve teaching in science, math and foreign languages. By the mid-1960s, attention shifted to the poor and disadvantaged in this country. Congress responded by enacting the Higher Education Act of 1965 which featured extensive aid

---

[13] See "College Recruiting," *E.R.R.*, 1974 Vol. II, p. 663.

for needy students and new programs of graduate study for public school teachers.

These programs plus the coming of age of the "baby boom" generation born after World War II resulted in a doubling of college enrollment in the 1960s—from 3,471,000 in 1959-60 to some 7,978,000 in 1969-70. Not only was there a large increase in the number of persons of college age, but the proportion going to college also rose. By 1970, 34 per cent of the 18-21 age group were enrolled in degree-credit programs in higher education, up from 23 per cent in 1960, 15 per cent in 1950 and 11 per cent in 1940.

Rising per capita income and growing social pressure to go to college contributed to the enrollment boom during the decade. Professor Paul Woodring, former education editor of the *Saturday Review*, wrote that a college degree had become a status symbol. "Both the students and their parents are convinced that the possession of such a document is essential if one is to achieve his goals in life." This belief, he added, "is rapidly becoming a part of the conventional wisdom. And to many the symbol has come to seem more important than the education it is presumed to represent."[14]

Job Shortages in Various Fields by Late 1960s

By the late 1960s, it had become evident that a college or graduate-level degree was not necessarily a ticket to a good job. Ivar Berg of Columbia University pointed out in his book *Education and Jobs: The Great Training Robbery* (1971) that almost four of every five college graduates were accepting jobs that had previously been filled by less-educated workers. A study by the Bureau of Labor Statistics in October 1972 showed that some 70,000 of the 750,000 persons who received college or graduate degrees the preceding June were unemployed. This was almost twice the national unemployment rate of 5.1 per cent. The study also showed that of those who found employment, many were in jobs virtually unrelated to their major studies in college. This situation applied to more than half of the humanities majors and to more than two-thirds of the business and social studies majors.

The very occupations that government programs had encouraged young people to enter a few years earlier were particularly hard hit. Unemployment or underemployment in science, engineering, teaching and business administration became apparent during the 1970 recession, the first since World War II in which large numbers of college-educated persons were thrown out of work. Toward the end of the year, 15 per cent of all business executives were estimated to be jobless. Due partly

---

[14] *The Higher Education in America: A Reassessment* (1968), p. 58.

to federal cutbacks in defense and space programs, 50,000 scientists and engineers were listed as unemployed in late 1970. Underemployment figures for these groups were believed to be considerably higher.

More publicized was the lack of job opportunities for teachers, particularly with doctoral degrees. Because of an anticipated decline in the number of professors needed in the next decade and an increase in the number of new graduates with Ph.D.s who wish to teach in college, their employment situation is not likely to improve. Many will be forced, like others immediately ahead of them, to find careers outside of academe. Some will compete for the dwindling number of teaching jobs in elementary and secondary schools. Others will settle for part-time teaching assignments which, according to Jane T. Flanders, a part-time lecturer in English at the University of Pittsburgh, "are marginal, expendable, underprivileged and underpaid."[15] Still others will try to find suitable work in private industry or government and, if all else fails, take temporary employment driving taxi cabs or tending bar. The majority will almost certainly be underemployed.

"Until we tell them [our young people] that it is hopeless to look for fulfillment in most of the jobs that are available to them, we will be fooling them."

Chifton Fadiman, Council for Basic Education

The problems facing college graduates were summed up by William K. West, a 28-year-old graduate school dropout who recently lost his job at the New York City Planning Commission. "I've been overtrained for every job I've held, so eight years at a university cannot be justified in terms of the inculcation of skills necessary for work," he wrote. "Unfortunately, the society seems to have developed a whole class of people like me." Society, he continued, has produced "an entire class of intellectual day laborers, either out of work or severely underemployed —the mandarins who never were, more casualties of the misplaced optimism of the Sixties, of faulty social engineering."[16]

---

[15] Quoted by Malcolm G. Scully in *The Chronicle of Higher Education*, Jan. 20, 1975.
[16] Writing in *The New York Times*, June 18, 1975.

These men and women are not likely to take much comfort from President Nixon's Labor Day address to a joint session of Congress on Sept. 6, 1971: "No work is demeaning or beneath a person's dignity if it provides food for his table and clothes and shelter for his children."

Proposals to Relieve Underemployment

CAREER EDUCATION—training for the world of work—is seen by many as the best answer to the problems of underemployment and unemployment. The term "career education" was coined by former U.S. Commissioner of Education Sidney P. Marland in 1971. The goal of such training, Dr. Marland wrote in *Career Education: A Proposal for Reform* (1974), was that "all young people upon leaving the educational system...should be ready immediately to enter satisfying and useful employment in a field of the individual's choice."

Career-education proponents are quick to point out that the concept is much broader than the old vocational-training idea, which concentrated on giving potential high school dropouts the kind of skill that could lead to jobs in machine work or carpentry. In their view, career education should begin in elementary school where young people would be made aware of the world of work and given some idea of what a career involves. High schools would be structured to permit students some on-the-job experience.

The new vocationalists also favor the increasing number of on-the-job programs on college campuses. According to the National Commission for Cooperative Education, 900 four-year colleges now provide work-study programs, compared to only about 40 a decade ago. Almost 200,000 students are currently participating in these programs. With jobs scarce and unemployment high, career education has wide appeal. But criticism of both the practical and philosophical aspects of the concept has also grown.

In a book entitled *Public and Proprietary Vocational Training: A Study of Effectiveness* (1974), Welford W. Wilms of the University of California Center for Research and Development found that only about 20 per cent of the post-secondary vocational graduates who had trained for professional jobs found work in their field. Those who were hired earned 36 per cent less than non-vocationally trained college graduates doing

Career Education Boom

The number of secondary and post-secondary students and adults enrolled in vocational programs increased from 12 million in fiscal 1973 to almost 15 million the next year, according to the American Vocational Association. In fiscal 1973, the latest year for which figures have been broken down, 7.3 million participated in high school career courses, 1.3 million in post-secondary programs and 2.6 million in adult classes.

the same work. Another difficulty with career training was summed up by Henry M. Wriston, president emeritus of Brown University, in *The New York Times* on June 11, 1975: "Technology, and scholarship for that matter, move so swiftly that old jobs become obsolete and new ones arise for which specific 'preparation' is not available."

The Council for Basic Education objects to the tendency of career-education advocates to define education solely in terms of work. "Should only the student who has chosen the science career...study science?" the Washington-based council asked in its February 1975 *Bulletin.* "And what about history, foreign languages, mathematics and all the other subjects that we believe all young people should study? Must the school find a clear connection between these and the student's career goal to justify their place in his program?.... We believe that the sound goals of education far transcend a person's intended occupational career."

The differences between career and basic educators are not as irreconcilable as they might seem. The careerists are not advocating the substitution of specific market skills for basic learning; they want a combination of both, suited to the student's ability and career preferences. Basic educators believe that specialization should be built on top of a broad, liberal base and that needed skills can often be learned more easily on the job than in the classroom. They also contend that since there are not enough good jobs to go around, a well-rounded education can help workers make better use of their leisure time.

Attempts to Make Employment More Satisfying

"Society must rid itself of the delusion that the major purposes of education are to serve the economy and the economic needs of students," James O'Toole wrote. "Failure to do so will not only exacerbate the problems of underemployment; it will lead to a serious compromise of educational institutions."[17]

---

[17] "The Reserve Army of the Underemployed," Part II, *Change,* June 1975, pp. 60-61.

16

O'Toole sees underemployment as a continuing and incurable problem in the developed world and suggests several ways of relieving the dissatisfactions common among underutilized workers.

These include more flexible working conditions, job retraining and greater opportunities for part-time work and self-employment. Experiments in job flexibility have focused on the four-day week,[18] less structured working hours, more employee autonomy and increased participation in the decision-making process. Social psychologist Lars E. Björk described a 1971-72 experiment in flexible working conditions in a Swedish machine assembly plant in the March 1975 issue of *Scientific American* magazine.

"Most of us have jobs that are too small for our spirits."

Woman worker quoted by Studs Turkel
in *Working* (1974)

The traditional system, in which each of 12 men performed one specific operation, was replaced by a system in which the workers could allocate individual tasks, learn other jobs and use whatever methods they found most convenient and satisfying to complete the work. Björk reported an increase in productivity after the new system was installed. While admitting that work satisfaction is subjective and therefore difficult to measure, he concluded that "perhaps the most obvious sign of increased satisfaction is the fact that none of the men wanted to go back to the old system."

Some American companies are making greater use of part-time workers, sabbatical leaves and early retirements to lessen worker discontent and increase productivity. Particularly on routine jobs, part-timers are less prone to boredom and fatigue and therefore less likely to make errors. Pitney-Bowes of Stamford, Conn., which manufactures machines, postage meters and credit cards, allows two part-time workers to share one job. Xerox lets its employees take a year or two away from their jobs to work in public-service employment. Such innovations may well make some jobs less boring but it is questionable whether

---

[18] See "Four-Day Week," *E.R.R.*, 1971 Vol. II, pp. 607-626.

> ## Graduates and Jobs
>
> "A statistical 'oversupply' of college graduates does not imply that college graduates will experience significant levels of unemployment. The unemployment rate of college graduates has always been lower than that of workers with less education. Problems for college graduates will center on underemployment and job dissatisfaction."
>
> —Bureau of Labor Statistics, "Occupational Outlook for College Graduates, 1974-75," 1974

they significantly reduce underemployment, particularly in white-collar occupations.

A growing number of workers are seeking to avoid underemployment and job dissatisfaction by going into business for themselves. Commenting on the increase in the number of young people starting new companies, Dora Dreiband of the New York County Clerk's Office said: "The youngsters just out of college, who are talented and well-educated, seem frustrated. Many don't feel like sitting around collecting unemployment or doing unskilled labor. So now the gutsy ones have been coming in a lot" to register to open a new business.[19]

Paradox of Job Openings Amid Unemployment

In addition to its public-service and manpower-training programs, the government has set up other projects to help the unemployed or underemployed find suitable jobs in their fields. Since 1968 the Department of Labor has operated Job Banks to compile lists of job openings and make the information available to city and state employment agencies. Even now, many available jobs go unfilled because of location, skill requirements or the unappealing type of jobs offered. Employment centers around the nation are reporting that droves of jobless work-seekers would rather continue to draw unemployment benefits than accept work they consider poorly paid, demeaning or beneath their ability.

At the same time, employers are reluctant to hire an "overqualified" applicant for fear that the person will quit the job at the first opportunity. Or they find that if a better job does not become available, the employee's frustration and unhappiness is likely to permeate his or her work and perhaps will soon be shared by other workers. In a survey of job opportunities around the nation published in The New York Times on July 1, 1975, Robert Lindsey wrote: "In a curious paradox of the nation's

---

[19] Quoted by Lawrence C. Levy in The New York Times, Feb. 23, 1975.

worst employment market since the nineteen-thirties, thousands of jobs go begging." He quoted Dorothy Graves, manager of the Southwest Pennsylvania Job Bank, as saying: "Anybody who is hard up and needs a job to eat can get work, even if they have no skills." But many of the jobs pay less than unemployment benefits and are regarded as menial or subservient.

Better methods for matching workers to jobs and improved forecasting are likely to have more of an effect on unemployment than on underemployment. The government now forecasts a slight increase in joblessness in the next few months and then a gradual reduction to about 8 per cent by the end of 1976. James O'Toole predicts that "whereas unemployment in the traditional sense will probably disappear in the U.S. in the future, the broader issue of underemployment will become more acute for all social classes because trends toward labor intensity and zero economic growth are likely to lead to a greater number of routine jobs."

Underemployment relief can come about in two basic ways. The first is the creation of many more good jobs that would use the skills and knowledge of an increasingly well-educated work force. The second, and probably more feasible, is a revolutionary change in the concept of work which might include greater job flexibility, options for career change and opportunities to move in and out of the labor force with more freedom than is now possible. If, as expected, the problems of underemployment and worker dissatisfaction grow in the years ahead, these and other alternatives are likely to be given more attention.

Unemployment in Two Decades

Sixties	Rate*	Seventies	Rate*
1960	5.5%	1970	4.9%
1961	6.7	1971	5.9
1962	5.5	1972	5.6
1963	5.7	1973	4.9
1964	5.2	1974	5.6
1965	4.5	Jan. 1975	8.2
1966	3.8	Feb. 1975	8.2
1967	3.8	Mar. 1975	8.7
1968	3.6	Apr. 1975	8.9
1969	3.5	May 1975	9.2
		June 1975	8.6

*Unemployment as a precentage of employment; monthly rates in 1975 are seasonally adjusted.
SOURCE: U.S. Bureau of Labor Statistics

Selected Bibliography

Books

Berg, Ivar, *Education and Jobs: The Great Training Robbery*, Praeger, 1970.

Ginzberg, Eli, *Manpower Agenda for America*, McGraw-Hill, 1968.

Howe, Irving (ed.), *The World of the Blue-Collar Worker*, Quadrangle Books, 1972.

Levitan, Sar A. and Garth L. Mangum, *Federal Training and Work Programs in the Sixties*, Institute of Labor and Industrial Relations, 1969.

Okun, Arthur M. (ed.), *The Battle Against Unemployment*, W.W. Norton & Company, 1965.

O'Toole, James, et al., *Work in America* Massachusetts Institute of Technology Press, 1973.

Turkel, Studs, *Working*, Pantheon, 1974.

Articles

Björk, Lars E., "An Experiment in Work Satisfaction," *Scientific American*, March 1975.

The Chronicle of Higher Education, selected issues.

Collins, Randall, "Where Are Educational Requirements for Employment Highest?" *Sociology of Education*, fall 1974.

Monthly Labor Review, selected issues.

O'Toole, James, "The Reserve Army of the Underemployed," Pt. I and II, *Change*, May and June, 1975.

"Planning for Full Employment," *The Annals* of the American Academy of Political and Social Science, March 1975.

Shaeffer, Ruth G., "The Buyers' Market for New College Grads," *The Conference Board Report*, February 1975.

Tussing, A. Dale, "Emergence of the New Unemployment," *Intellect*, February 1975.

Werther, William B., "Part-Timers: Overlooked and Undervalued," *Business Horizons*, February 1975.

Reports and Studies

Bureau of Labor Statistics, U.S. Department of Labor, "Expenditures and Manpower Requirements for Selected Federal Programs," 1975.

—"Occupational Outlook for College Graduates, 1974-75," 1974.

Carnegie Commission on Higher Education, "College Graduates and Jobs: Adjusting to a New Labor Situation," April 1973.

Council for Basic Education, selected reports.

Editorial Research Reports, "Education for Jobs," 1971 Vol. II, p. 845; "Inflation and Job Security," 1974 Vol. II, p. 707.

Gaines, Rilford, "Unemployment," Economic Report of the Manufacturers Hanover Trust Company, April 1975.

Keyserling, Leon H., "Full Employment Without Inflation," Conference on Economic Progress, prepared for the Task Force of the Commission on Full Employment, January 1975.

National Academy of Sciences, "Forecasting the PhD Labor Market: Pitfalls for Policy," April 1974.

U.S. Departments of Labor and Health, Education, and Welfare, "Manpower Report of the President," April 1975.

R ETIREMENT SECURITY

by

Helen B. Shaffer

1 9 7 4
D e c. 27

RETIREMENT SECURITY

R ECESSION AND INFLATION, the twin horrors of the current economic situation, are stirring new fears among those whose working years are nearing an end. The reason is that their prospect for a reasonably comfortable income in retirement—an expectation nurtured by maturation of the Social Security system, growth of private pension plans, and rising interest on savings—no longer seems quite so secure as in the immediate past. While recent increases in Social Security benefits, partly tied to rises in the Consumer Price Index, help meet the inflation threat, payments to many beneficiaries are still no match for the cost of living.

There are other threats arising out of the overall economic situation: the declining value of pension trust funds and personal holdings because of the stock market slump; rising unemployment which deprives pensioners of extra-income odd jobs and reduces payments into public and private pension funds; and the expected cutback of government expenditures for public services utilized by the elderly.

It is no wonder that the trend toward early retirement, which had been building up in recent years, has begun to slow down as older workers cling to their jobs as long as possible.[1] On the other hand, where unemployment is most severe, the retiree on fixed income may be the most favored member of his community. An ironic situation may develop in which the meagerly but regularly paid pensioner will be helping to feed the young, able-bodied worker unable to find a job.

Even if the decline in economic activity should reach depression levels, the factor of retirement will make a vast difference between the current situation and that of previous depressions, as during the 1930s. For retirement as a status has become of great significance both in the personal lives of the people and the economic structure of the nation. Currently some 38 million Americans receive regular cash payments based on public retirement programs sponsored by the U.S. government. At least 1.5

---

[1] See "Early-Retirement Bait Loses Much of Its Lure As the Economy Sags," *The Wall Street Journal*, Nov. 11, 1974.

million others receive regular payments under retirement systems for state employees.

Effect of Retirement Programs on U.S. Economy

The sizable segment of the nation's population in retirement status *(see box, p. 34)* gives the elderly leverage to impress their needs on political and social policymakers. Economic questions concerning the aged have to do not just with the adequacy or inadequacy of their public benefits but the capacity of the nation to support, out of past savings and current income, a growing part of the citizenry that is economically non-productive. Many economists, for example, point out that Social Security benefits are given at the expense of low-wage earners. Since 1950, Social Security benefits have increased as follows:

Effective	Per cent	Effective	Per cent
September 1952	12½	January 1970	15
September 1954	9	January 1971	10
January 1959	7	September 1972	20
January 1965	7	March 1974	7
February 1968	13	July 1974	4

Regular cost-of-living increases in Social Security benefits were mandated under 1972 legislation and were revised a year later. Under current provisions of law, an increase of 3 per cent or more in the Consumer Price Index in the first quarter of the year above the first quarter of the previous year will require an automatic increase in benefits. To support the increases in benefits, the Social Security tax and the amount of earnings on which it is based have risen several times in recent years, as is shown below:

Year	Annual maximum taxable earnings	Tax rate, employer and employee, each	Tax rate, self-employed
1970	$7,800	4.8%	6.9%
1971	7,800	5.2	7.5
1972	9,000	5.2	7.5
1973	10,800	5.85	8.0
1974	13,200	5.85	7.9
1975*	14,100	5.85	7.9

Becomes effective Jan. 1

For the retired individual, the big question is how much confidence he or she can have that the system will in fact provide economic security in old age. So far the public programs have held up very well, though at levels of benefits and coverage that have still left many old people in poverty. The private pension system, far less extensive since it is voluntary, has worked well for some but fallen down for others. Some but not all of the private pension system's failings were attended to when President Ford on Sept. 2 signed the Employee Retirement Income Security Act of 1974, popularly known as the pension reform bill *(see pp. 35-38).*

Persistence of Aged Poverty Despite Improvement

On the whole, the economic condition of retirees and their dependents or survivors has greatly improved over what it was in the past. However, despite a current annual expenditure of possibly $100 billion in public and private "transfer" funds—pensions, disability benefits, public assistance, etc.—for the support of the elderly, there remain millions of old people who live in poverty and neglect.

A Brookings Institution analysis of the federal budget shows that in the current fiscal year, $86.8 billion is being spent by the government for cash income and maintenance programs directed entirely or in great measure to the benefit of the old and the retired of all ages. In addition $28.6 billion is being spent for "helping people buy essentials," as in housing and food-stamp programs. One-half of this sum ($14.2 billion) is the outlay for Medicare.[2] Private systems add another increment; in 1970 the private pension outlay to 4.7 million persons was $7.4 billion.

The growth of these expenditures—Social Security payments alone having risen from $11 billion in 1960 to $64.4 billion in 1975—obviously had much to do with the reduced incidence of true poverty among the elderly. According to the Brookings study, "the incidence of poverty was cut in half [during the 13-year period, 1959-1972], as the number of people over 65 rose and the number of *poor* old people declined [from 5.7 million to 3.7 million]." Among the millions who have been saved from poverty by these programs, however, are many retired persons engaged in a desperate struggle to keep from losing the minimal security and independence for which they have worked and saved during their economically productive years. The truism about the elderly today is that those who were poor before retirement are even poorer afterward, and many who were well-off before retirement become poor afterward.

The average monthly payment under Social Security for a retired worker in July 1974 was $186.71 and for a disabled worker $204.68. The most that a worker who retires in 1974 may get is only a shade over $300. The maximum for those who retired in earlier years is less because the monthly benefit is

---

[2] Barry M. Blechman, Edward M. Gramlich, and Robert W. Hartman, *Setting National Priorities: The 1975 Budget* (Brookings Institution, 1974), p. 168.

based on the average of annual pay on which a Social Security tax was paid. In earlier years the level of pay that was taxed was lower than it has been in more recent years. If the retired person is living with a dependent spouse, the benefit amount is increased by 50 per cent.

The insufficiency of the typical Social Security payment to meet the cost of living is indicated by hypothetical budgets developed by the Bureau of Labor Statistics for a retired urban couple. At last accounting, in the autumn of 1973, the bureau said average costs, excluding personal income taxes, amounted to $3,763 "at a lower level of living," $5,414 at an "intermediate level," and $8,043 at a "higher level." Since then the Consumer Price Index has risen about 12 per cent.[3] Furthermore, these hypothetical couples are presumed to be in reasonably good health and able to care for themselves, which is not true of all the elderly.

Social Security as Major Source of Cash Income

Obviously the success of the system relies on the retiree's possession of other resources. A Social Security Administration study of private pension plans indicated that approximately 15 per cent of all aged couples or single persons receiving Social Security payments were also deriving support from private pension plans. The sums available from that source tended to be smaller than from Social Security.

Generally speaking, families that draw private pensions are better off than those that do not. Most of the private pension systems were in major and highly unionized industries where pay scales were relatively high and job security was strong. Beneficiaries therefore were favored not only by receiving the extra monthly check but by their relatively high Social Security payments based on their past earnings. These industries included manufacturing, transportation, communications, and public utilities.[4]

All studies of the economic condition of the older American point to the preponderant importance of the Social Security benefit in providing cash support for the retirement years. A government survey of the situation in 1967 indicated that Social Security benefits "were virtually the only source of retirement income...for more than one-half of the aged married couples getting benefits and nearly two-thirds of the non-married aged beneficiaries."[5]

[3] The increase from November 1973 to November 1974 was 12.1 per cent.

[4] Walter W. Kolodrubetz and Alfred M. Skolnik, *Pension Benefit Levels: A Methodological Analysis* (Social Security Administration, Office of Research and Statistics, Staff Paper No. 1, 1972).

[5] Social Security Administration, *Social Security Programs in the United States* (1973), p. 22.

Another report based on data from this survey indicated that one-half of the married couples had less than $2,000 in assets and two-thirds of the single persons had less than $1,500. "Clearly a majority of the elderly could not have counted on much income from such savings," the report concluded. Home ownership was common, especially among the married couples, 77 per cent of whom owned at least an equity in their homes while four-fifths of the homeowning group had already paid off the mortgage.[6] But many older persons lack the means to keep their homes in repair and they are often the victims of rising property taxes or deteriorating neighborhoods.

The black old person is more likely to be poor than his white counterpart. Special census surveys in 1972 indicated that 40 per cent of the 1.6 million blacks above age 65 were living in officially defined poverty, in contrast to 17 per cent of the 20.1 million whites in that age group.[7] The blacks were less likely to have other assets or second pensions and their benefits under Social Security were lower because of lower earnings in their working years.

Impact of Inflation on Fixed Incomes of the Aged

The big obstacle to retirement security is inflation. The current inflation is described by the Federal Reserve Board as "the most severe and prolonged that the United States has experienced since the rise in prices following World War II."[8] The 1973 rate of price increase was double that of 1972 and further acceleration of the rate occurred in 1974. The Consumer Price Index rose faster in the first 10 months of 1974 (10.6 per cent) than it did in the entire 12 months of 1973 (8.8 per cent).

Inflation has hurt the retired person and his family in more ways than one. The chief thrust, of course, is the rise in prices of basic necessities. Food, shelter, medical care and transportation account for at least four-fifths of old people's budgets at lower and moderate levels of living, according to the Bureau of Labor Statistics. Food prices in November 1974 were 11.9 per cent higher than 12 months earlier. Transportation costs were up 14.0 per cent, housing 13.6 per cent, and medical care 11.8 per cent.

Inflation hurts in another way by the pressure it puts on governments to curtail social services. These services are often more vitally needed by the elderly than other persons. In terms of medical care, inflation hits the elderly not only in the purchase of medicines, eyeglasses, foot and dental care, and

---

[6] Janet Murray, "Homeownership and Financial Assets: Findings from the 1968 Survey of the Aged," *Social Security Bulletin,* August 1972.

[7] Bureau of the Census, *Supplementary Report on the Low-Income Population: 1966 to 1972* (Current Population Reports: Consumer Income, Series P-60, No. 95), July 1974, pp. 2-3.

[8] "Recent Price Developments," *Federal Reserve Bulletin,* September 1974, p. 613.

other cost items not covered by Medicare, but it has forced the government to increase the amount charged directly to the retiree for hospitalization[9] and the amount charged to him or her for insurance against physician fees. Inflation also puts pressure on workers to fight for wage increases, a fight in which the blows fall ultimately on the person of fixed income. Such struggles may lead to strikes, depriving the public of accustomed services that are more essential to the older segment of the population than to others.

When transit workers struck in Los Angeles in October 1974, many persons in that automobile-oriented city managed to adjust to the deprivation reasonably well. But for the elderly, the loss of bus service was devastating. Many could not drive or did not own cars and lacked the strength to walk long distances to grocery stores, doctors' offices, churches and banks. Some of those who could walk the necessary distances were afraid of being attacked and robbed; slow-moving elderly persons are targets for muggers.

"The big obstacle to retirement security

is inflation."

The economic handicaps of the retiree are somewhat modified by various benefits granted senior citizens. These include no federal tax payments on their Social Security benefits, a double tax exemption on other income they receive, plus reduced fares on many transit systems during non-rush hours, discounts on tickets for shows and concerts, and various social services such as home-delivered meals, free transportation and visiting nurse services. The development of these programs has been encouraged by the availability of federal funds for this purpose, dating from the establishment of a federal agency, the Administration on Aging, under the Older Americans Act of 1965. These programs were expanded by Older Americans Comprehensive Services Amendments of 1973.

A majority of the states now provide some property tax relief to homeowners and renters among older or low-income persons. California, Colorado, Connecticut, Georgia, Iowa, Kansas, Michigan, Missouri, Nebraska, South Dakota, Virginia and

---

[9] The amount the Medicare patient must pay for hospitalization—the "deductible"—will rise on Jan. 1, 1975, to $92—up from $40.

Wisconsin are among the states that have adopted some form of "homestead tax relief" or have liberalized previous enactments to this effect.[10] A bill introduced in Congress by Sens. Edmund S. Muskie (D Maine) and Charles H. Percy (R Ill.) would provide federal reimbursement to states for one-half of the property tax relief offered low-income homeowners and renters.

Growth of Public and Private Pensions

PENSIONS ORIGINATED many centuries ago as personal grants by royalty to favored individuals. The choice of beneficiary was arbitrary. Those favored might be ex-ministers or ex-mistresses, and the amounts given were equally subject to royal whim. One of the excesses of the *ancien regime* wiped out by the French Revolution was an overgrown system of pensions to court favorites that made a heavy drain on the public treasury. This system was replaced by new principles that "involved a recognition of the public obligation to assist by pension, on the basis of definite rules, any persons, irrespective of station, who had been employed by the public authorities and had become incapacitated after long and faithful public service or in consequence of an injury sustained in it, or any other citizen who had sustained sacrifices in the service of society."[11]

Formal pension systems were first instituted for ex-soldiers, then extended to other public employees. The practice of establishing private pension funds, supported by employer and employee, began to take hold during the latter part of the 19th century. Almost from the start, the principle prevailed that employees as well as employers should contribute to systems that promised to provide for workers in their old age.

A corollary of this principle was that the pension benefit was no longer to be viewed as a benefaction bestowed by the mighty on the worthy, but a deferred wage to which an aged or disabled worker was entitled as a matter of right after a lengthy period of service. Employers were induced to accept the obligation to contribute to these plans on the theory that workers would accept a lower wage and remain with the same firm, despite tempting offers from other places of work, in order to qualify for the retirement benefit. The pension thus came to be regarded as a contractual obligation.

[10] Council of State Governments, *Book of the States 1974-75*, p. 393.
[11] "Pensions," *Encyclopaedia of the Social Sciences*, Vol. 12 (1934), p. 66.

Growth of Social Security Benefit Payments

Average Monthly Cash Benefits*

	Number of Beneficiaries	Retired Worker	Dependent Spouse	Children	Widows
1940	222,000	$ 22.60	$12.13	$ 9.70	$ 20.28
1950	3,462,000	43.86	23.60	17.05	36.54
1960	14,811,000	74.04	38.72	28.25	57.68
1965	20,867,000	83.92	43.63	31.98	73.75
1970	26,229,000	118,10	61.19	44.85	101.71
1974	30,122,000	179.30	91.42	66.40	169.53

*As of December each year except 1974, when May figures apply

SOURCE: Social Security Administration

As time went on, greater emphasis came to be placed on attainment of a certain age. However, length of service continued to bear on the amount due a worker on retirement. As pension systems grew, the need for sounder financing became apparent and this led to the introduction of actuarial expertise in devising the financial structure of the systems.

Origin and Growth of U.S. Social Security System

The first major public system of social insurance against old age dependency was introduced in Germany in 1889. Other nations of Europe soon followed suit. The United States was one of the last of the modern industrial nations to introduce such a plan. Twenty-seven other countries already had established well-developed national retirement systems.

From the beginning of social insurance in the United States, a double motive prevailed—that of alleviating poverty and of replacing earned but withheld income. It is significant that the federal social insurance system and the public assistance system were born in the same piece of legislation—the Social Security Act of 1935. The need for both programs had long been apparent, but it was the magnitude of the economic crisis of the 1930s that compelled Congress to authorize so radical a turnabout of social policy.[12] The practical necessity at that time was to create purchasing power for millions who were unable to obtain the barest necessities of life.

The 1935 act created three new systems: (1) retirement in-

[12] Not so radical, however, as the then-popular Townsend Plan, sponsored by Dr. Francis E. Townsend, a California physician, which called for a flat payment of $200 a month—more than the average paycheck at that time—to every person 60 years or older in the nation.

surance for persons presumed too old to work,[13] (2) unemployment insurance for those temporarily unable to find work, and (3) public assistance for the poor who, for reasons beyond their control (disability, infirmities of old age, blindness, responsibility for the care of young children) were unable to seek work.

Social Security began almost solely as an insurance system and it still retains many features of such a system. The 1935 act required that employer and employee in commerce and industry pay 1 per cent each on the first $3,000 of the worker's wages. The money was placed in a trust fund from which future benefits to retirees would be drawn. The system was given until 1942 to accumulate enough to begin paying out benefits. It was not long, however, before Congress began to amend the act in order to extend benefits on the basis of social need rather than merely earned right.

Changes Since 1935 to Raise and Extend Benefits

The first cluster of amendments, adopted in 1939, made the first benefits payable in 1940, revised the benefit formula to increase minimum payments, and made certain dependents of retired workers and survivors of deceased workers eligible for benefits too. The 1939 amendments also established the principle of a minimum income for aged retirees; payments were to be based on the average monthly wage rather than on the size of the accumulated wage during a lifetime. The result, according to a Brookings Institution study, was that "the principle of individual equity was severely modified...to attain other welfare-oriented goals."[14]

The "social adequacy" principle gained emphasis as the amendments piled up over the years. Coverage was extended until the system became all but universal. Benefits, tax rates and the taxable pay base were raised repeatedly. Most significantly, benefits were made available to numerous beneficiaries on the basis of social need rather than on their past contributions to the system. An amendment adopted in 1950 not only extended coverage to additional categories of workers, but made it possible for workers who were to retire in 1954 to qualify for full benefits after only 1½ years of covered employment.[15]

Benefits were extended to the disabled at age 50 in 1956, to the dependents of the disabled in 1958, and to all disabled persons regardless of age in 1960. Meanwhile, in recognition of the inade-

---

[13] A secondary motive was to encourage older workers to retire and make way for younger workers in a job-short labor market.

[14] Joseph A. Pechman, Henry J. Aaron, and Michael K. Taussig, *Social Security: Perspectives for Reform* (1968), p. 33.

[15] After 1954, the required period of coverage was to rise step by step until 1971 when 10 years of work history would become the basic requirement for eligibility to receive benefits.

quacy of earned benefits to meet the cost of living, the retirement test—meaning the amount of money a retired person may earn before forfeiting at least part of his retirement benefit—was liberalized step by step. The original act provided benefits only to persons who received no earnings at all. The 1939 act permitted earnings up to $15 a month without loss of benefits. Beginning Jan. 1, 1975, a retired person may earn up to $2,520 a year or $210 a month before he or she forfeits $1 of each $2 earned above those limits.

When the Social Security Act was adopted, it was hoped that as the social insurance system matured, the need for public assistance for the aged would shrink to a residual few. Instead, the numbers on Old-age Assistance rolls grew. This situation has been attributed to the inadequacy of Social Security benefits despite the increases, to inflation, and to shrinking earnings of older workers in an era of technological change. By early 1953, some 2.7 million old people were receiving welfare cash benefits. The number did decline after that, however. By December 1973, the last month of Old-age Assistance before aid-to-the-indigent-aged was to be taken over by a new program, the number on OAA rolls was 1,820,000.

New Program of Assistance to the Aged Poor

The new program of assistance to the aged poor is known as Supplemental Security Income (SSI), authorized by the Social Security Amendments of 1972, effective Jan. 1, 1974. The 1972 Amendments have been described as a "major landmark in a period of extraordinary activity in the area of Social Security legislation," and of all the provisions in the amendments SSI was said to constitute "the most revolutionary shift in the Social Security structure."[16]

SSI constitutes, in all but name, a guaranteed annual income for the aged, the blind and the disabled. It provided originally for at least $130 a month for a single person and $195 a month for a married couple. [17] Those amounts were later raised, effective July 1974, to $146 and $219. Social Security Amendments of 1973 also made SSI recipients eligible for Medicaid, the federally aided, state-administered health service for persons who cannot afford to pay their own medical expenses.

Unlike the old OAA, SSI is fully financed by the federal government from general revenues; OAA had been a joint federal-state

---

[16] Robinson Hollister (associate professor of economics, Swarthmore College), "Social Mythology and Reform: Income Maintenance for the Aged," *The Annals of the American Academy of Political and Social Science*, September 1974, p. 27.

[17] If the individual or couple received more than 20 additional dollars from another source (including Social Security) or $65 in earnings, SSI benefits would be reduced by 50 cents for every dollar of income received above these amounts.

program. This means that there is a nationally uniform floor for the aged, the blind and the disabled, rather than various standards set by states. Minimum payments under SSI are higher than the former OAA maximums in about half of the states. The new program is under the Social Security Administration, which expects to provide benefits in 1975 to more than five million persons, most of them elderly, compared with 3.2 million under the entire state-federal public assistance program that preceded it.

The result of these developments is a greater intermingling of the welfare benefit concept with the insurance principle. Of the 29.9 million people receiving benefits in December 1973 under the Old-age, Survivors, Disability and Health Insurance program—that is, the basic Social Security insurance system—only 15.4 million were retired workers, 62 or older, whose benefits were based on contributions from their earnings during their pre-retirement years. Two million were the disabled who qualified at a younger age, and the rest were wives, widows, children, parents, and a special group of individuals 72 or older who had been brought into the benefit system though not qualified on the basis of contributions to the system.

Recent Growth of Private Pensions in America

The years of Social Security expansion were also years of growth for private pensions. In 1940 only four million employees were covered by private pensions; estimates of the number now run up to 35 million or roughly one-half of the industrial work force.[18] Collective bargaining had much to do with this growth.

According to a study by the Joint Economic Committee of Congress: "In the mass-production industries, union pressure converted pensions from the practice of a few of the 'enlightened' employers into a mass phenomenon; in other industries, especially among small firms, the presence of the union made the difference between pensions and no pensions. Once coverage was established, the unions worked steadily to improve the terms of the plan."[19] Coverage under collective bargaining was also spurred by the *Inland Steel* decision of 1949 in which pension plans were declared to be a proper subject of collective bargaining.[20]

---

[18] This may be an exaggerated estimate. A special survey jointly sponsored by the Social Security Administration and the Departments of Labor and Treasury indicated that in April 1972 approximately 23 million full-time wage and salary workers were covered by private retirement plans. It was suggested that higher estimates might have failed to take account of much dual coverage. See Walter Kolodrubetz, "Employee-Benefit Plans, 1972," *Social Security Bulletin*, May 1974, pp. 15-16.

[19] Joint Economic Committee, *The Labor Market Impact of the Private Retirement System*, October 1973.

[20] This federal appeals court ruling, Inland Steel v. National Labor Relations Board (170 F. 2d 247), was in effect upheld by the Supreme Court in 1949 when the Court refused to review the case.

America's Retired Population

One American in every ten today has passed his or her 65th birthday, the standard milestone for retirement. The 1970 Census counted more than 20 million persons in this older age bracket. Not all were retired, however; some older persons were still at work. And a number of persons had retired before they reached 65—often at age 62 when many become eligible for reduced benefits.

The retirement period is likely to last a number of years. Men at age 65 may, statistically, look forward to 13.1 more years of life; women at 65 may look forward to 17.2 more years. When death occurs, cash benefits continue to flow to the surviving spouse and dependent children.

Of the 30.1 million persons now receiving Social Security benefits, 10.6 million are under 65. Most of these younger recipients are wives or widows of retired workers or they are dependent children or disabled offspring of the primary retiree. Some 3.7 million of the younger group are themselves retired or disabled. Benefit claims may be made at any age if the disability is severe enough.

Tax benefits also encouraged the growth of pension plans. In plans that meet Internal Revenue standards, employers may deduct their contributions to the pension funds and wage earners do not pay taxes on their contributions until they receive the benefits in retirement. They are then likely to be in a lower tax bracket. The Life Insurance Company Income Tax Act of 1959, by permitting tax deduction on earnings of invested pension funds held by insurance companies, provided another growth incentive. The Self-Employed Individuals' Retirement Act of 1962—the so-called Keogh Act[21]—permitted the self-employed to place part of their earnings in a retirement plan and defer paying taxes on the amounts until retirement.

As the plans grew, so did concern for the security of the systems. This concern sharpened considerably in 1964 when the Studebaker automobile plant in South Bend, Ind., closed down and terminated its pension plan, affecting the retirement security of 10,500 workers. At the time, 3,600 persons were already retired or eligible to retire. A distribution of the $25 million fund to meet these obligations left 4,000 vested[22] employees between the ages of 40 and 60 with the prospect of receiving only 15 per

---

[21] Named for Rep. Eugene J. Keogh (D N.Y., 1937-1967), who sponsored the legislation.

[22] A vested worker has fulfilled stipulated requirements, usually a given number of years on the job, to receive a partial or full pension at retirement age even if he is no longer under the plan.

cent of their vested rights, while 2,900 other workers under the age of 40 could expect nothing.

There followed a decade of extensive congressional investigation of private pension plans by several committees and a presidential committee.[23] These studies showed, Sen. Harrison A. Williams Jr. (D N.J.) told the Senate, Aug. 22, 1974, that "too many workers, rather than being able to retire in dignity and security after a lifetime of labor rendered on the promise of a future pension, find that their earned expectations are not to be realized."

According to Treasury records, in 1972 alone, 19,400 workers lost their rights to approximately $49 million in potential pension benefits because the plans were terminated without enough funds to meet obligations. After many efforts to devise legislation to protect worker interests and compromises on divergent views, the Employee Retirement Income Security Act of 1974 was approved and signed into law on Labor Day. This act represents a new major step in government regulation of private pension systems.[24] Its impact is yet to be determined.

Prospects for More Retirement Security

HOW SECURE IS the retirement future of the American worker? The current recession and inflation make all predictions precarious, but on the whole the safeguards for a solvent retirement would appear far stronger today than they have ever been and they are likely to grow stronger. Several factors account for this view: the broadened coverage of Social Security to near-universality, the improvement of Social Security benefits, the incorporation of income-floor and cost-of-living-increase provisions into the benefit system, the growth of private pensions, the growing size of the older population with its added political clout, and the growth of effective senior-citizen lobbying groups.

A major advance in retirement security is expected to result from the new Employee Retirement Income Security Act. Sen.

[23] President's Committee on Corporate Pension Funds and Other Private Retirement and Welfare Programs, whose report, *Public Policy and Private Pension Programs*, was issued in January 1965. The congressional committees were: Senate Committee on Labor and Public Welfare, Senate Finance Committee, House Committee on Ways and Means, House Committee on Education and Labor, Joint Economic Committee, Senate Special Committee on Aging, and Joint Committee on Internal Revwnue Taxation.

[24] The Welfare and Pension Plans Disclosure Act of 1958 required plan administrators to file annual reports on the structure and operations of the funds. Its central idea was that disclosure alone would be sufficient to maintain the financial integrity of pension plans.

Jacob K. Javits (R N.Y.), a leading sponsor of the legislation, described it as "the greatest development in the life of the American worker since Social Security." "For the first time in our history," he added, "most workers will be able truly to retire at retirement age and to live decently on their Social Security and private pensions." The legislation was made necessary, he added, by "the absence of any supervision" over private pension funds, representing assets in excess of $160 billion, and "the lack of minimum standards to safeguard the interests of plan participants and beneficiaries." Major provisions of the law are:

Vesting. Plans must include any employee who has reached the age of 25 and has had at least one year of service.[25] Employers may choose one of three procedures for vesting.

Funding. Contributions must be made at a rate sufficient to provide reasonable assurance that adequate funds will be on hand to meet pension obligations.

Insurance. A Pension Benefit Guaranty Corporation in the Department of Labor will provide insurance to meet pension obligations in case funds are short. Employers will pay $1 into the insurance fund for every covered employee (50 cents for multi-employer plans).

Management. Standards for management of pension funds were established and limits set on transactions that might involve conflict-of-interest.

Individual Pension Accounts. Individuals not covered by a pension plan may establish their own retirement accounts with contributions that are tax-deductible. The tax-free amounts that the self-employed may contribute to their own retirement accounts (as previously provided by the Keogh Act) were raised from a maximum of $2,500 a year to $7,500, or 15 per cent of income, whichever is less.

The fiduciary standards, reporting and disclosure provisions become effective Jan. 1, 1975. The law provides for delay, until January 1976, for application of the participation, vesting and funding standards to plans in existence on Jan. 1, 1974.

From the standpoint of retirement security, the greatest weakness of the private pension system is beyond the reach of legislation. It is that the plans fail to cover one-half of the employed population. Since private pension plans remain voluntary, there is nothing in law to prevent employers from terminating them, so long as they meet the obligations already incurred at the time of termination.

---

[25] This is partial vesting. For 100 per cent vesting, the 25-year-old could be required to have three years of service, with service before age 25 counting toward the three years. For details of the act's provisions and its legislative history, see *Congressional Quarterly Weekly Report*, Aug. 24, 1974, pp. 2326-2327, and "Pension Reform: the Long, Hard Road to Enactment," *Monthly Labor Review* (Department of Labor magazine), November 1974, pp. 3-12.

Beneficiaries of Federal Retirement Programs*

Programs	Retired and Disabled Workers and Dependents	Survivors
Social Security*	23,106,000	7,163,000
Railroad retirement	655,000	335,000
Civil Service	943,000	371,000
Veterans	3,243,000	2,295,000
Subtotals	27,947,000	10,164,000
Total	38,111,000	

*Statistics as of July 1974 except for Civil Service and veterans' survivors, which date from June 1974

**Old-age Survivors and Disability Insurance

SOURCE: Social Security Administration

The promoters of pension regulation were disappointed that the act did not include a strong portability provision to permit workers to carry full pension rights as they moved from one job to another. "While this legislation does remove some of the restrictions [on portability]...it does not entirely free an employee from the need to stay at one place of employment for a certain length of time...in order to have his credits vested," complained Rep. Michael J. Harrington (D Mass.).

Some critics object to what they consider favoritism toward the upper-income brackets in tax and pension laws. The complaint is that corporations get appreciable tax relief from contributions to pension systems that assure their top-level executives princely incomes on retirement.[26] An amendment offered to the pension bill by Sen. Gaylord Nelson (D Wis.) would have set a limit of $45,000 on annual retirement income from tax shelter sources. It failed to win approval.

An amendment that was adopted, the one that increased the amount the self-employed can put away tax-free, is seen as a boon to pensioning for the rich. An article in *Barron's,* a business weekly, hailed the amendment as favoring independent businessmen and professional persons of high income. The author drew up a hypothetical case of a self-employed individual in the 50 per cent tax bracket who puts aside $7,500 a year over a 15-year period, invested at 8 per cent, for pension purposes. Under the new rule, the tax-free $7,500 annual contribution and

[26] See Robert N. Schoeplein, "Pension Reform for the Rich," *The Progressive,* March 1974, pp. 36-39.

its tax-free earnings would amount to $203,640 at the end of the 15-year period. If the $7,500 and its earnings were taxable, the individual would have saved only $3,750 a year and his accumulation in 15 years, according to this accounting, would be only $67,825.[27]

Questions About Viability of Retirement Systems

Other questions are raised about the viability of the pension system as a whole. Writing in *Harvard Business Review*, Robert D. Paul, head of a pension consulting firm in New York, suggested that the prevailing form of private pension plans, which base benefits on averages of peak earning years, may be outmoded. "Their structures may not be suited to the kind of economy we now seem to be entering," he wrote, "and the cost...may increase to unsupportable heights." While pension plans may have worked well during periods of low inflation, they "may not fit the economy of the 1980s and 1990s."[28]

In addition, the aging portion of the population will put a larger burden of support on the producing population; the proportion of the population above 65, 9.8 per cent in 1970, is projected to rise to 10.9 per cent in the year 2000 and 13.1 per cent in 2020. The growing tendency of women to pursue full-time career employment will deprive the pension funds of contributions from the wages of women as casual employees—contributions which in the past have been forfeited by women for lack of sufficient credits to qualify for benefits.

Another point is that industry is likely to give in to the demands of women liberationists for equal treatment with men as pensioners, even though women tend to live longer in retirement and hence would make heavier drains on the funds than men if their monthly benefits were the same. Still another factor is the trend in collective bargaining toward lowering the age of retirement and toward inserting cost-of-living escalations in benefit schedules. Both of these features have been incorporated into public retirement systems, including Social Security.

The doleful prospect envisioned for private pensions is matched by the forecasts of pessimists regarding the future of the Social Security system. The latter foresee a financial collapse when the cost of the system becomes too great a burden on the tax-paying worker. Several factors, they point out, will account for a coming imbalance in the tax-benefit ratio. One is that the size of the population in retirement will grow relative to the size of the population drawing taxable income. Another

[27] Steven S. Anreder, "Win with Keogh: The New Pension Law Greatly Aides [sic] the Self-Employed," *Barron's*, Oct. 7, 1974, p. 3. See also *The Wall Street Journal*, Dec. 17, 1974.
[28] Robert D. Paul, "Thinking Ahead: Can Private Pension Plans Deliver?" *Harvard Business Review*, September-October 1974, pp. 22-34, 165.

factor is that benefits are based on taxable earnings in the years immediately preceding retirement, which are usually much higher than in most of the years when the retiree was contributing to the system. Adding to the tax burden are the liberalized benefits, including built-in cost-of-living increases. Thus the outgo from the Social Security fund may rise to insupportable heights.

The Board of Trustees of Social Security trust funds has made the following projections of the system's income-and-disbursement experience over the next 75 years: for the first 25 years, slowly increasing costs relative to income; for the second 25 years, rapidly increasing costs; for the third period, high but leveled-off costs amounting to about 17.68 per cent of payroll (compared with the present 10.44 per cent). The board emphasized that accuracy in such projections is hard to achieve. Factors affecting future costs include economic developments, changes in the cost of living, increases in disability awards at early ages, changes in labor force participation, unemployment rates, average earnings, and future fertility rates.[29]

Emergence of New Breed of Retired Persons

Some believe it is time to dispense with what they consider the fiction of social insurance and convert Social Security in name and in fact to a general welfare program for the aged. This would silence complaints that the Social Security tax is regressive, applying disproportionately to low-wage earners. The alternative would be to make retirement payments out of general revenues and dispense with the entire concept of a trust fund.

Imminent changes of this nature are not expected. The labor movement and the increasingly influential senior citizens' societies are adamantly opposed to such a change and it is not likely that the American worker is as yet willing to embrace the idea that his retirement pay will be in the form of a gratuity rather than an earned right. Change is more likely to come by grafting on more welfare features—such as the existing ones of weighting benefits to provide a floor for the poorest recipient—and injecting some general funding to provide social services.

What may change the entire picture is that a new breed of retiree is coming to dominate the scene—a person who is less work-worn, better educated, more sophisticated in the ways of government, better cushioned financially, and with a better background of nutrition and medical care than his predecessor of even 10 or 20 years ago.

---

[29] Board of Trustees of the Federal Old-age and Survivors Insurance and Disability Insurance Trust Funds, *1974 Annual Report*, referred to the House Committee on Ways and Means, June 3, 1974 (House Document No. 93-131).

Selected Bibliography

Books

Blechman, Barry M., et al., *Setting National Priorities: The 1975 Budget*, The Brookings Institution, 1974.
Pechman, Joseph A., et al., *Social Security: Perspectives for Reform*, The Brookings Institution, 1968.
Council of State Governments, *Book of the States, 1974-75*, 1974.
Booth, Philip, *Social Security in America*, University of Michigan Institute of Labor and Industrial Relations, 1972.

Articles

Anreder, Steven S., "Win With Keogh: The New Pension Law Greatly Aides [sic] the Self-Employed," *Barron's*, Oct. 7, 1974.
Ball, Robert M., "Social Security Amendments of 1972: Summary and Legislative History," *Social Security Bulletin*, March 1973.
Henle, Peter, and Raymond Schmitt, "Pension Reform: The Long, Hard Road to Enactment," *Monthly Labor Review*, November 1974.
Irelan, Lola M., "Retirement History Study: Introduction," *Social Security Bulletin*, November 1972.
Kolodrubetz, Walter, "Employee-Benefit Plans, 1972," *Social Security Bulletin*, May 1974.
Paul, Robert D., "Thinking Ahead: Can Private Pension Plans Deliver?" *Harvard Business Review*, September-October 1974.
Schoeplein, Robert N. "Pension Reform for the Rich," *The Progressive*, March 1974.
Tussing, A. Dale, "The Dual Welfare System," *Society*, January-February 1974.

Reports and Studies

Bureau of the Census, *Money Income in 1973 of Families and Persons in the United States* and *Supplementary Report on the Low-Income Population: 1966 to 1972* (Current Population Reports: Consumer Income, Series P-60, No. 93 and No. 95), July 1974.
Department of Labor, "Three Budgets for a Retired Couple, Autumn 1973," news release, Aug. 27, 1974.
Editorial Research Reports, "Social Security Financing," 1972 Vol. II, p. 705; "Plight of the Aged," 1971 Vol. II, p. 865.
House of Representatives, "Employee Retirement Income Security Act of 1974, Conference Report" (Report No. 93-1280), Aug. 12, 1974.
President's Committee on Corporate Pension Funds and Other Private Retirement and Welfare Programs, *Public Policy and Private Pension Programs*, January 1965.
Senate Finance Committee, Subcommittee on Private Pension Plans, "Private Pension Plan Reform," hearings, Parts 1 and 2, 1973.
Senate Special Committee on Aging, "Developments in Aging" (Report No. 93-846), May 13, 1974.
Senate Subcommittee on Labor, Committee on Labor and Public Welfare, "Private Welfare and Pension Plan Study, 1972: Report on Hearings of Pension Plan Terminations," September 1972.
Social Security Administration, *Social Security Programs in the United States*, 1973.

40

CONSUMER CREDIT ECONOMY

by

David Boorstin

**1 9 7 5
Apr. 11**

CONSUMER CREDIT ECONOMY

T HE AMERICAN WAY OF LIFE is built on debt. Hundreds of billions of dollars' worth of credit have enabled Americans to enjoy cars and refrigerators, furniture and fashionable wardrobes, hospital care and vacations, and a host of smaller purchases. Consumer credit[1] stood at $21.5 billion in 1950. As of Feb. 28, 1975, the figure was $185 billion, and nearly 80 per cent of all American consumers were using credit in some form, ranging from department store charge accounts to home-improvement loans. By stimulating demand, this growth in consumer credit has spurred the production of goods and services on a mass scale. No other country in the world has such a big, rich economy, and no other economy has such a reliance on personal debt—some $900 worth for every man, woman and child in the United States.

But now the nation's troubles are shaking the foundations of its credit economy. Rising prices have inflated the people's borrowing needs but have slashed the share of income available to them to pay their debts. At the same time recession has taken its toll in jobs and salary expectations, reducing even further the people's ability to repay what they owe. Yielding to this pressure, Americans have reduced their net borrowing by record amounts. A record contraction of $877 million occurred in December 1974, and January 1975 was the third consecutive month in which outstanding consumer debt decreased. Never before had consumer debt fallen for three months in a row.[2] In February, the latest figures showed, installment lending increased by $237 million—spurred by the auto industry's cash-rebate sales campaign—but non-installment credit fell for the fifth consecutive month.

But while consumers have been trying harder than ever to get out of debt, a growing number of them are going under. Personal bankruptcies during the second half of 1974 were 103,216, almost

[1] Consumer credit, as defined by the Federal Reserve Board, excludes some $600 billion in mortgages. Total debt in the United States amounts to $2.8 trillion, including $1.3 trillion in corporate debt, $500 billion in U.S. government debt, and $200 billion in state and local government debt.

[2] The last time consumer debt fell for two consecutive months was in May and June 1958, and the previous record for a single month was a $376 million contraction in June 1972.

one-third more than in the second half of 1973, and the Bankruptcy Division of the U.S. Courts expects a record number of filings in 1975: by one estimate, 225,000.

Those who supply credit, as well as those who use it, have been forced into a re-evaluation. The high cost of money made lenders tighten the credit reins last year, and now the growing number of defaults has led them to be even more cautious. The Installment Lending Division of the American Bankers Association reported a record delinquency rate at the end of 1974, as did Master Charge with its 34 million credit-card holders. John Reynolds, president of Interbank Card Association, which is the licensor of Master Charge, expressed the feelings of many bankers and other lenders when he said: "We can't give credit out like before."[3]

Above all, credit represents confidence—confidence on the part of lenders that they will be repaid, and confidence on the part of consumers that they will be able to meet their obligations. The spectacular expansion of consumer credit in the last quarter-century took place because Americans had high expectations about the future. This encouraged them to enjoy today what they would pay for tomorrow. Thus the strain on consumer credit represents more than just another set of statistics: it is an important signpost, among the 12 leading indicators used by the Department of Commerce's Bureau of Economic Analysis. Gordon R. Worley, vice-president for finance of Montgomery Ward & Co., has said: "It's an early warning sign.... It's never failed us yet."[4] The willingness to borrow against their own future reflects Americans' expectations about the future of "the American way of life."

Questions About Availability and Use of Credit

Credit has become more than just a convenience, enabling consumers to "buy now, pay later." It is a major marketing tool. Any reduction in consumer credit has great implications for industries geared to installment debt. Automobile loans account for one-third of all installment credit, and in an effort to boost lagging sales and soften the impact of rising car prices, the automobile finance companies have been extending their credit terms longer than ever, to 48 months.[5] Consumers' willingness to go into debt also directly affects the sales of large appliance manufacturers and large retailers.

---

[3] Quoted in *Business Week*, Feb. 17, 1975, p. 47.

[4] Quoted in *Business Week*, Oct. 12, 1974, p. 96.

[5] According to one study, an American keeps a car for an average of 4.1 years. Thus extended financing could lead in the long term to a leveling off of car sales, as buyers hold on to their cars longer.

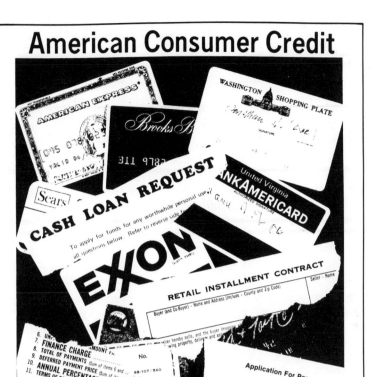

American Consumer Credit

Four out of five American consumers use credit in some form...

Consumer credit, currently $185 billion, has risen ninefold in the past quarter-century...

Faced with a recession, consumers borrow less...

But more of them go bankrupt... A record number of bankruptcies is expected this year.

Financial institutions have also encouraged the use of personal credit. Many banks now offer "no-bounce" checking plans with open lines of credit, and cash advances on credit cards. Finance companies advertise widely and encourage borrowing by mail. In the words of one promotional pamphlet, "The best things in life *aren't* free.... Just decide how much money you want. Fill out the brief application we've enclosed. Mail it back to us...and upon approval, your money will be sent to you by return mail."[6]

In their sometimes aggressive willingness to grant credit, either for its own sake or as a tool to get sales, lenders have been

---

[6] Government Employees Financial Corporation, an affiliate of Government Employees Insurance Corporation (not affiliated with the U.S. government).

accused of pressuring consumers into overextending themselves. Chairman William Proxmire (D Wis.) of the Senate Banking Committee, who has long been concerned with consumer finance, has said: "We aren't serving any social purpose by making credit available to everybody. There are millions who can't handle credit. They look at it as an Aladdin's lamp they can rub, and their lives are ruined by it."[7]

The congressionally established National Commission on Consumer Finance acknowledged in its 1972 report that "The desire of credit grantors to provide credit and the eagerness of consumers to acquire goods and services financed with credit may, indeed, lead consumers to use credit to excess." But, the report added, "forces operate to counteract over-reliance on credit," in particular the natural caution of lenders and borrowers, and "analysis of aggregate data does not indicate a dangerous situation of overindebtedness."[8]

However, according to a survey undertaken for the commission, overextension was second only to unemployment as the most important reason cited by creditors for the failure of debtors to meet their obligations. And according to another study quoted in the commission's report, certain groups are particularly liable to find themselves in trouble: "The greatest proportion of debtors in trouble were found among the unmarried (especially the separated, divorced and widowed), the poor, and those under 25 or 65 years and older.... About 40 per cent of single-person households and Negro households were, by our definitions, in deep trouble."[9]

Recently, credit counseling offices have experienced a rush of clients. The non-profit National Foundation for Consumer Credit (NFCC), which offers help to the financially overextended at 170 offices nationwide,[10] counseled 142,000 families in 1974, a 30 per cent increase over the previous year. Of that number, 56,-000 went into debt-management programs; these 56,000 families had debts totaling $370 million. "And for every family who com-

---

[7] Quoted in *The Christian Science Monitor*, Sept. 11, 1974.

[8] "Consumer Credit in the United States," Report of the National Commission on Consumer Finance, December 1972, pp. 17-21. The commission was established under the Consumer Credit Protection Act of 1968, which also included the provisions of the Truth in Lending Act. The nine members, appointed by Congress and the President, supervised a staff of more than 30.

[9] Mary E. Ryan and E. Scott Maynes, "The Excessively Indebted, Who and Why," *Journal of Consumer Affairs* (1968), pp. 107-126, cited in "Consumer Credit in the United States," pp. 19-20.

[10] NFCC affiliates are known as Consumer Credit Counseling Services. Most of them are autonomous, community-supported agencies. Some are partially funded by the federal government or are associated with municipal authorities or local charitable institutions. No more than 40 per cent of the members on their governing boards may represent the credit-grantors of the community. Under debt-management programs, debtors are helped to increase their income if possible, reduce their expenditures, and budget carefully. At the same time, counselors undertake to arrange with creditors for reduced payments of manageable proportions.

Consumer Credit Since 1950, by Type

(in billions of dollars)

Type of credit	Feb. 28, 1975	Year end				
		1970	1965	1960	1955	1950
Total consumer credit	185.4	127.2	89.9	56.1	38.8	21.5
Installment	152.7	102.1	70.9	43.0	28.9	14.7
Automobile	50.9	35.2	28.4	17.7	13.5	6.1
Other consumer goods	50.1	31.5	18.5	11.5	7.6	4.8
Home improvement	8.0	5.1	3.7	3.1	1.7	1.0
Personal loans	43.7	30.3	20.2	10.6	6.1	2.8
Non-installment	32.7	25.1	19.0	13.2	9.9	6.8
Single-payment loans	12.6	9.7	7.7	4.5	3.0	1.8
Charge accounts*	8.5	8.0	6.4	5.3	4.8	3.4
Service credit**	11.6	7.5	4.9	3.3	2.1	1.6

* Includes retail charge accounts, service station and "travel and entertainment" credit cards and home heating oil accounts. Retail credit cards and bank credit cards are included in installment loan figure under "other consumer goods."

**Mainly amounts owed to doctors, hospitals, and utilities.

Figures may not add up to totals because of rounding.

SOURCE: Federal Reserve Board and *Statistical Abstract of the United States* (Department of Commerce, 1974)

es to see us," an NFCC spokesman told Editorial Research Reports, "there are another six or seven who don't know where to go." Another increase of at least 30 per cent is expected in 1975.

A new breed of debtor is emerging, younger and more prosperous, driven to the brink by expensive but easy credit coupled with the onset of double-digit inflation. Bank credit cards pose a new problem. While total consumer debt outstanding decreased from November 1974 to January 1975, bank credit card debt rose by half a billion dollars. The psychological difference between having to apply for a loan and having an open line of credit on a bank card has apparently led consumers to borrow on their credit cards even as they are trying to reduce their other debts.

Even the well-to-do have been using credit cards to tide themselves over. "When the bill comes," the NFCC spokesman said, "people are afraid to find out how much they owe, so they just pay the minimum and don't even look at the total—which keeps growing." Some credit-business executives have admitted that they made credit too accessible in the past. The aggressive marketing of credit, and the inability of some consumers to cope with the temptations thrust upon them, have made the great expansion of credit appear a mixed blessing to many.

While the ready availability of credit has posed problems for some consumers, for others it is the barriers to credit that are threatening. In a society where credit is so pervasive, an individual's lack of credit or a credit record can be a severe handicap. Yet lenders must be able to distinguish between good and bad credit risks, and this requires that they make distinctions on the basis of past experience with various categories of borrowers. If lenders are not discriminating enough, their debt losses will mount, and customers who repay their debts will be forced to subsidize those in default. On the other hand, if credit grantors are overly cautious, they will turn away good accounts along with bad, and will lose business to competitors who can more accurately identify good credit risks.

Problems of Discrimination in Credit-Granting

Credit discrimination is criticized for two reasons. First, it penalizes applicants who are in a "high-risk" category but who are not high risks themselves. Second, some discrimination may not be warranted by statistical evidence. Women have been the primary victims of unfair credit discrimination. "Most banks have a long history of treating women as 'second-class citizens' (particularly when it comes to loan and mortgage applications)," according to *Business Week*.[11] At its hearings in May 1972, the National Commission on Consumer Finance was told of difficulties faced by women seeking consumer and mortgage credit. These complaints generally fell into five categories:

1. Single women have more trouble obtaining credit than single men.

2. When a woman marries, creditors generally require her to reapply for credit, usually in her husband's name—regardless of whether or not she maintains the same job, salary, or bank account. Similar reapplication is not asked of men when they marry.

3. Creditors are often unwilling to extend credit to a married woman in her own name.

4. Creditors are often unwilling to count the wife's income when a married couple applies for credit.

5. Women who are divorced or widowed have trouble establishing or re-establishing credit. Women who are separated have a particularly difficult time since the accounts may still be in the husband's name.

Jane Roberts Chapman of the Center for Women Policy Studies in Washington, D.C., wrote, "Relatively few women have their own credit records or economic identity....Good credit ratings

---

[11] *Business Week*, Jan. 12, 1974, p. 76.

...become the property of the husband, regardless of how faithfully the wife contributes to...that record."[12]

In the last two years considerable progress has been made in the area of sex discrimination. The Equal Credit Opportunity Act of 1974, which takes effect in October 1975, prohibits discrimination against credit applicants on the basis of sex or marital status. Pressure, publicity and legislation notwithstanding, many women feel that credit discrimination against them will not end until lenders are convinced that they can handle credit as well as men can—or even better—as several studies have confirmed.[13] Women seek to disprove the traditional notions that they are financially dependent on men, or, if of child-bearing age, are likely to become pregnant and drop out of the work force. The proportion of all women who work has grown to 42 per cent; 13 million, over one-third of the female labor force, work even though they are mothers of children under 18 years of age.

Controversies Over Screening and Collection

Parallel to the growth of consumer credit has been the growth of agencies that report on a potential borrower's credit history. Some 2,600 credit bureaus across the country now furnish over 100 million credit reports annually. An additional 30 to 40 million investigative reports are made yearly for employers and insurance companies. An individual's "credit rating" has become ever more important in determining his economic status. A single inaccuracy, locked into the information system, can have a serious effect on his life. But until a few years ago, consumers had no right to discover what was on their record. The Federal Fair Credit Reporting Act of 1970 was the first significant national effort to give consumers the chance to find out and correct erroneous information about them.

Unfortunately, after thousands of complaints to the Federal Trade Commission, it has become clear that the act is not succeeding. Sheldon Feldman, the FTC's assistant director for special statutes, said the act "is unintelligible and frustrating to consumers, and those actions taken to comply by reporters or users have fallen short of what consumers consider reasonable under the circumstances. The entire procedure...has proven to be

---

[12] Jane Roberts Chapman, "Women's Access to Credit," *Challenge*, January-February 1975, p. 41.

[13] According to Chapman: "One retail trade association analyzed the accounts of six large department stores and found that 6.6 per cent of the accounts held by single women became delinquent, compared with 8.4 per cent for those of single men. A study in the mid-1960s...found that bad-account probability for both married and single women was substantially lower than that for men with the same marital status.... Not one lending institution interviewed during the Center for Women Policy Studies credit project reported a higher rate of default on the credit extended to women than to men."

ineffective."[14] Senator Proxmire, the author of the act, feels that it needs strengthening to (1) give consumers physical access to, or copies of, their files, (2) give consumers a better idea of what information in their files has led to a credit rejection, (3) require the person's permission before investigating his private life, and (4) allow the consumer to bring common-law action for damages against reporting agencies and sources for defamation, invasion of privacy, or negligence.

The act requires only that the agency provide an oral disclosure of the "nature and substance" of a file, which, according to Federal Trade Commission Chairman Lewis A. Engman, has often led to "wholesale withholding of information."[15] The withholding of information was one accusation in a formal complaint the FTC has filed against Retail Credit Co., largest of the investigative agencies, which operates 1,700 offices, annually makes 35 million reports for 85,000 customers and maintains files on 48 million people.[16] When credit agencies do disclose information, it is often found to be incomplete and out of date, as *Business Week* correspondents around the country reported upon checking their own files.[17]

With the growing number of delinquencies brought about by the nation's economic problems, there has also been increasing concern about some tactics used by creditors and the collection agencies they hire. These have included harassment, intimidating phone calls made at unusual hours, and threats of violence or defamation. A stream of horror stories moved the New York State Legislature to pass a debt-collection-procedures act that went into effect in September 1973. "The law has helped tremendously, but the economy is such that the law notwithstanding, there is an increase in harassments," according to Richard A. Givens, director of the FTC's New York office. In recent months his office has received 100 complaints a month, twice the previous rate.[18]

---

[14] Sheldon Feldman, "The Fair Credit Reporting Act—From the Regulators Vantage Point," *Santa Clara Lawyer* (law journal of Santa Clara University), Vol. 14, 1974, p. 471.

[15] Testimony before the Senate Consumer Credit Subcommittee in October 1974, quoted by Sen. William Proxmire, "Consumer Credit: Privacy the Collateral," TRIAL, January-February 1975, p. 36.

[16] In an administrative proceeding such as this, the FTC seeks to obtain a "consent decree" under which the accused consents to "cease and desist" from specified practices. Retail Credit was accused, among other things, of not having adequate means to ensure the accuracy of its reports, setting daily report work loads so high that its employees must falsify information to meet quotas, and requiring its investigators to file a certain number of derogatory reports.

[17] *Business Week*, Dec. 7, 1974, p. 97.

[18] Quoted in *The New York Times*, Feb. 16, 1975.

Development of Lending Practices

THE LENDING OF MONEY is one of the world's oldest professions, and contemporary society's views on the subject have their origins in ancient times. The biblical injunction against usury, as interpreted by the Christian Church, profoundly affected modern Western attitudes toward credit. The biblical doctrine was simple: do not take back more than is given.[19] Interest was declared a punishable offense in 789, subject to excommunication in 1179, and its prohibition superseding all civil laws to the contrary in 1311. Usury was branded a mortal sin, the most vehement condemnation and the most powerful deterrent the Church could employ. The medieval poet Dante reflected this attitude in his *Divine Comedy*, wherein he assigned usurers to one of the most uncomfortable circles of Hell.

However, despite the official position, "It goes without saying that the rich and the trading classes found devices to circumvent these canon laws even during the height of the Church's power in the Middle Ages."[20] The problem was partially one of semantics, for the term usurer was generally used to refer to all profiteers, and the Church's position was aimed not just at moneylending but at all kinds of business extortion. The pressures for credit were too great for the enforcement of artificial prohibitions against the taking of any interest. Merchants, lords and kings required loans, and their needs were met one way or another. The Church itself, as one of the richest and most influential institutions in Europe, developed intricate financial affairs involving the great Italian banking families, lending, borrowing, and enmeshing itself in a practice it condemned.

The turning point came in the latter half of the 16th century, when non-profit pawnshops, jointly managed by clergymen and municipal officials, were established for the benefit of the poor. To cover the operating costs of these charitable agencies, the papal sanction was obtained for charging low rates of interest on their loans. This was a significant break in the rigid definition of usury as the taking of *any* return for the loan of money. Theologians soon came to reason that the lender should be compensated not only for his expenses but also for his cost of

---

[19] Leviticus 25:35-37: "And if thy brother be waxen poor, and fallen in decay with thee...take thou no usury of him, or increase..." and Deuteronomy 23:19-20: "Thou shalt not lend upon usury to thy brother; usury of money, usury of victuals, usury of anything...."

[20] Irving J. Michelman, *Consumer Finance: A Case History in American Business* (1966), p. 90.

capital—the return he could have earned by placing his funds in investments of similar risk. Now usury was redefined as the taking of excessive interest, rather than the taking of any interest.[21]

Adoption of English Lending Practices in America

Interest ceilings were established in England by Henry VIII, who set them at 10 per cent; by 1714 the figure had been halved. The 13 American colonies, with the exception of New Hampshire, followed this example and established their own maximum interest rates. They took care, however, to make them just enough higher than 5 per cent to attract British investment in the colonies. These 18th-century rates remain in many U.S. state laws and constitutions today—even though the English repealed all their usury statutes in 1854.[22]

Credit was an accepted fact of life in the colonies, not just for the merchants and importers who relied heavily on credit from their British suppliers, but for their customers. Retail credit was available to farmers on a crop-to-crop basis, with the finance charge implicit in the price of the goods. Thomas Jefferson, heavily in debt himself, wrote in 1787: "The maxim of buying nothing without the money in our pocket to pay for it would make of our country one of the happiest on earth.... I look forward to the abolition of all credit as the only other remedy."[23] Yet even such an apostle of thrift as Benjamin Franklin is known to have extended credit liberally as a printer and bookseller.

A legal market for installment loans was effectively outlawed, however, by the usury laws that America had inherited from England. These prohibited moneylending at economically feasible rates. Jeremy Bentham, the prominent "utilitarian" philosopher of the day, as well as Sir William Blackstone, the premier legal expert, had pointed out the shortcomings of rate ceilings, and in particular the way in which too low a rate invited evasion. In 1834 over 200 Boston businessmen signed a petition urging the repeal of Massachusetts usury laws, citing the trading difficulties they caused and the "notorious" abuses. Two years earlier Abraham Lincoln, age 23, had reached the opposite conclusion: one plank in his platform for election to the Illinois General Assembly called for regulation of interest rates. At the same time, he sought to keep such a law from prohibiting a transaction above the ceiling rate in cases of extreme necessity.

---

[21] The Church finally approved of interest officially through pronouncements between 1822 and 1836, though it was not until 1950 that Pope Pius XII declared that bankers "earn their livelihood honestly." See Sidney Homer, *A History of Interest Rates* (1963), pp. 80-81.

[22] National Commission on Consumer Finance, *op. cit.*, p. 93.

[23] Quoted by Michelman, *op. cit.*, p. 98.

Many states deliberately weakened their usury laws, enabling high interest rates to prevail despite the strong opposition of western and southern farmers who, being debtors, wanted "cheap money." The agrarian movement in American politics, especially during the second half of the 19th century, advocated low interest rates along with such better publicized issues as the free coinage of silver and the use of greenbacks as legal tender. The centers of finance in the urban East had opposing views.

Growth of Unregulated Lending and Loan Sharks

The industrialization and urbanization of America worked some important changes in the consumer credit business. A class of wage or salary earners developed with enough margin above the bare necessities to enable them to handle credit transactions. In many states, salary loans were made possible by the assignment of part of the borrower's wages to the repayment of his debt. Lenders were virtually assured of repayment, since employers generally were firm believers in the sanctity of contracts and were liable to fire a worker who showed irresponsibility in his financial affairs. These salary loans tended to put borrowers chronically in debt, while the lender could claim exemption from the usury laws on the ground that he was not lending money, but simply purchasing a salary as one might purchase any other commodity.

The urban worker's regular flow of wages, as compared to the farmer's or farm-laborer's seasonal income, also made possible regular payments on an installment purchase. And other new forces were at work. Historian Daniel J. Boorstin has pointed out:

> Industry was using newly improved metals (especially iron and steel) to turn out millions of durable objects which nearly every citizen could imagine owning. Since a sewing machine could usually be reconditioned for the secondhand market, it did not seem imprudent for the retailer to allow a customer to use the machine while he paid for it.[24]

Similarly, durable mass-produced items made possible the chattel loan, a variation of the pawnbroking concept. In this case, the security was left in the hands of the borrower.

Salary loans were generally very small—$10 to $40—and chattel loans averaged only about twice as much. The size of the sums involved meant that lenders charged high rates in order to cover their overhead and make a profit that they saw as being commensurate with their risk. An investigative study published

---

[24] Daniel J. Boorstin, *The Americans: The Democratic Experience* (1973), p. 424.

by the Russell Sage Foundation in 1908 found that the average salary loan office in New York had only $10,000 out on loan, but charged interest at an annual rate of 120 to 240 per cent or even more. These rates were often accompanied by harsh collection practices.[25]

The flourishing illegal loan offices, which by 1900 were operating in almost every large city, bore witness to the need for small installment loans. Many of the borrowers were genteel but impoverished civil servants and members of the middle class who were unable to live on their meager incomes, especially when faced with medical bills or funeral expenses. Arthur Michelman, in his history of American consumer finance, noted that "even the loans of the unregulated lenders were better than no loans at all, and countless emergencies and hardships must have been solved by these loans in spite of their excessive charges." But public opinion of the time was almost as antagonistic toward the borrowers as toward the loan sharks who exploited them; newspapers criticized debtors as "victims of their own folly" and blamed them for mismanaging their financial affairs.

As well as fighting the loan sharks themselves, philanthropic organizations led by the Russell Sage Foundation sought to change these attitudes and to convince the public that there was a legitimate need for legal sources of consumer credit. Their efforts to attract responsible capital into the consumer finance field finally resulted in the drafting of a model Uniform Small Loan Act, eventually adopted by most states. It allowed regulated lenders to make small loans at rates in excess of the limits set by usury laws. Credit unions, which have become an increasingly important source of consumer credit, began operating in 1909, and Morris Plan banks in 1910.[26] The latter paved the way for commercial banks to take up installment lending, but this did not happen until much later. The National City Bank in New York was among the first to organize a personal loan department, in 1928.

Automobile Financing; Postwar Credit Explosion

It was the automobile that transformed installment buying into a dominant American institution. "Until automobiles came off the assembly lines by the millions there was no other object of universal use so costly as to require a scheme for time payments."[27] New techniques of buying and financing developed

---

[25] One favorite tactic used by loan offices was to send a female "bawlerout" to the delinquent debtor's place of employment, to denounce him loudly in front of his colleagues as a liar and a cheat.

[26] Named for Arthur J. Morris, who devised an ingenious method of avoiding the usury limits by a combination of a direct loan with a required installment deposit.

[27] Daniel J. Boorstin, *op. cit.*, p. 423.

Consumer Installment Credit Outstanding, Feb. 28, 1975

(in billions of dollars)

Holder	Total	Auto-mobile	Other con-sumer goods	Home improve-ment	Per-sonal loans
Commercial banks	71.2	29.6	21.9*	4.4	15.2
Finance companies	38.2	12.4	8.1	0.9	16.7
Credit unions	22.1	8.4	2.1	0.7	10.9
Miscellaneous lenders (Mutual Savings Banks, Savings & Loan)	3.1	0.2	0.1	2.0	0.8
Retail outlets	18.2	0.3	17.9	—	—
Total	152.7	50.9	50.1	8.0	43.7

* Includes $8.1 billion worth of credit cards.
Figures may not add up to totals because of rounding.

SOURCE: Federal Reserve Board

---

even more rapidly than the methods of automobile production, and provided both a mass market for cars and a remarkable increase in the volume of consumer credit. Ironically, Henry Ford opposed time-payment plans, favoring instead the old-fashioned virtues of thrift and prudence. Bankers, too, believed that automobiles ought to be paid for in cash, and in 1926 the American Bankers Association advised its members not to finance automobile installment purchases.

By the early 1930s the bankers had changed their minds, but by then buying an automobile with cash had become the exception rather than the rule: nearly 80 per cent of the three and a half million passenger cars sold in 1923 were bought on some kind of time-payment plan. This was made possible by the automobile finance firms, which originated in 1915 with the Guaranty Securities Company, organized by businessmen in Toledo, Ohio, to finance the purchase of Willys-Overland cars. By 1925, when automobile manufacturing ranked first among the nation's industries, there were more than 1,700 such finance companies.

General Motors had set up its own financing agency in 1919, and Ford changed its policy in 1928. As the auto industry came to be concentrated in a few companies, it lessened the risk that a manufacturer would go out of business before a car was paid for. The Soldiers' and Sailors' Civil Relief Act, which freed members of the armed forces from the need to make installment payments during World War II, led to fears among lenders that millions might interrupt their payments or turn in their install-

ment-purchased cars. But few did, and this established installment buying even more firmly after the war. From 1919 to 1963,
General Motors' Time Payment Plan had financed nearly 50
million car buyers.

The postwar credit boom was the result of consumer and
business adaptation to a changing way of life. America's increasingly urban population enjoyed a growing level of
"discretionary income" above what was needed for the
necessities of life, and as their expectations for the future grew,
so did their willingness to incur debt. Young married couples are
heavy users of credit, and the number of young people grew
faster than any other age group. With home ownership came
asset ownership—of stoves, refrigerators and television sets. As
more women moved into the labor force and the desire for
leisure time increased, there was an added demand for labor-
saving devices such as vacuum cleaners, dishwashers and self-
timing ovens.

---

*"Once in my life I would like to own
something outright before it's broken! ...I
just finished paying for the car and it's on
its last legs."*

Willy Loman in *Death of a Salesman* (1949)

These young people, with higher, more stable incomes than
their parents enjoyed at the same age, developed a greater
willingness to use credit. The credit industry responded by
creating new forms of consumer credit. Competing gasoline
companies and large retailers not only offered credit but made it
portable and convenient by introducing the credit card. This was
soon transformed into an all-purpose credit device. Beginning in
1950 the Diners' Club, followed by Carte Blanche and American
Express, made a profitable business out of supplying credit
cards and assuming the risk on credit-card accounts.

The Franklin National Bank of New York offered the first
bank credit card in 1951. In the late 1960s, in order to convince
retailers that enough persons held the cards to make it
worthwhile joining their plan, banks began mailing credit cards
unsolicited. This created high risks of fraud, and was prohibited
in 1970. But by then the embossed plastic chips had worked a

revolution in consumer finance: "Credit, once closely tied to the character, honor and reputation of a particular person, one of a man's most precious possessions, was becoming a flimsy, plasticized, universal gadget."[28] Today there are estimated to be 500 million credit cards of all kinds in use—more than two for every American.

Directions in Consumer Borrowing

A LARGE BODY of consumer law has evolved in recent decades, but public discontent with credit problems has not decreased. According to the National Commission on Consumer Finance, "A partial explanation of this phenomenon can be attributed to unsuccessful enforcement of these laws." It added:

> ...Governmental mechanisms for protecting consumers in the credit arena are incredibly diverse. Two planes of variables contribute to the confusion. First, some creditors are extensively regulated for consumer credit purposes while others are scarcely touched by regulatory agencies. Second, some creditors are regulated by federal authorities, some by state authorities, some by both, and some, in truth, by neither.

The reasons for this state of affairs lie in the history of the consumer credit industry, in which new credit grantors entered the field intermittently and credit legislation emerged on a piecemeal basis.

After almost a decade of controversy, Congress in 1968 enacted a "truth-in-lending" law—in the Consumer Credit Protection Act—to help consumers make informed decisions when they obtained credit.[29] One of the toughest and most far-reaching consumer bills passed by Congress since the securities disclosure laws of the 1930s, the heart of the bill was a requirement that all buyers should be told the cost of loans and installment purchase plans in terms of an annual percentage rate calculated in a specified way. The resulting uniformity was intended to let consumers make valid cost comparisons between the lending rates or installment plans of different stores or lending institutions, just as they could compare the prices of similar products manufactured by different companies.[30]

[28] *Ibid.*, p. 428.

[29] The first truth-in-lending bill had been introduced by Sen. Paul Douglas (D Ill., 1949-1967) in 1959. That bill and others introduced in the 87th, 88th and 89th Congresses all failed, but the 1968 bill included the essence of his earlier measures.

[30] See Congressional Quarterly's *Congress and the Nation*, Vol. II (1969), pp. 807-813.

In 1970, Congress restricted the issuance of unsolicited credit cards and limited to $50 a cardholder's maximum liability for unauthorized use of his or her card. The same law included provisions which for the first time regulated the activities of consumer reporting agencies. Further amendments in 1974 (1) sought to protect consumers against inaccurate and unfair credit-billing and credit-card practices, and (2) banned discrimination on the basis of sex or marital status from any credit transaction.

Controversy remains over the proper scope for federal regulation of consumer credit. The ancient question of whether rate ceilings are desirable—and if so, at what levels they should be set—is still being asked, and tight credit conditions have also led to proposals for credit allocation in order to relieve certain credit-starved areas of the economy such as housing, small business, and state and municipal governments.

The growth of consumer credit has also led economists to consider controls on it as a tool of monetary policy. "The mountainous private debt is a potential weak link in the economy," the *Journal of Commerce* observed June 11, 1974. "It could be the weakest link." Some experts feel that selective controls over the terms of consumer credit—controls affecting the volume of new credit extended and/or the level of credit repayments—might aid attempts at overall economic stabilization. Others argue that controls on consumer credit would not help the whole economy, and they fear giving government officials power to decide what consumer expenditures are appropriate. The revival of interest in selective controls reflects the disappointment and disillusionment of many economists with the performance of general monetary policies.

While the Board of Governors of the Federal Reserve System controls interest rates paid on different types of savings accounts, and the money supply in general, it does not set interest rates on loans or control the volume of consumer credit. During World War II and the Korean War it did have such authority, which it exercised, but Congress chose to let this authority lapse in 1952. The Credit Control Act of 1969 gave the President power to regulate and control all types of credit through the Federal Reserve Board, but this power has never been used.

Credit Cards; Approaches to a Cashless Society

Credit cards were originally seen as a customer service, rather than as a revolutionary change in the method of payment. But it has become clear that they are nothing less than revolutionary. Bank credit cards in particular, although they constitute only a

The Bank-Card Question

Bank credit cards furnish the smallest consumer loans in the business. They have other unique characteristics as well: both assumption of debt and repayment occur more at the discretion of the debtor than is true of other forms of consumer debt, and the cards are used to buy a widening variety of goods and services.

But their increased use has created new problems. Bank cards offer an ever-open line of credit up to a certain limit. Thomas Russell suggested in *The Economics of Bank Credit Cards* (1975), "there operates in credit card use a law similar to Parkinson's law...that expenditure expands to use up lines of credit extended." This has led to fears that some consumers—especially those whose financial status prevents them from getting cheaper loans elsewhere—are drawn into overextending themselves as they would not do if they had to apply for personal cash loans for the same amount.

While it is not in a bank's interest for its credit-card holders to go bankrupt, it is definitely to the bank's advantage that they use their cards generously and—moreover—that they incur finance charges by not paying their bills in full within a specified period. The profitability of bank credit cards hinges on usage patterns instead of just credit-worthiness. Low-risk, high-income cardholders are likely to use them as a convenient way to avoid carrying cash, rather than as a source of credit, presumably because they can qualify for lower-cost loans.

On the other hand, according to a study by Dr. Elick N. Maledon Jr. and Conway T. Rucks published in *The Journal of Consumer Credit Management* in its summer 1974 issue: "Lower-income cardholders tended to use the credit aspect of the card more frequently and, consequently, provided more revenue per capita than the higher-income convenience users. Admittedly, it follows that these same cardholders will generate more costs in terms of collection effort and bad debt experience but, so long as the marginal costs do not exceed the incremental revenues, a positive profit contribution exists."

In the current recession, banks may make credit cards less available. But in the long run, according to this study, it is in the banks' interest to maximize the profit of their credit-card programs by encouraging more low-income consumers to go into debt.

fraction of the hundreds of millions of charge cards in existence, have tremendous implications for the future.

The use of bank credit cards has increased at a continuous and rapid rate. From virtually nothing in the mid-1960s, debt created by such cards has grown to $8.3 billion, or 5.4 per cent of all installment credit. In 1974 alone, outstanding credit-card debt increased by 22 per cent, and the trend is expected to continue. This growth has not always meant profits from credit-card programs for the banks involved, since there have been considerable start-up costs, fraud losses, and expense involved in serving cardholders who are "convenience" users rather than credit users *(see box, p. 59)*.[31] But banks also fear to remain outside the credit card system, because it is widely viewed as the forerunner of the Electronic Funds Transfer System (EFTS). The research and development of the bank credit-card system has substantially prepared the way for EFTS—more commonly known as the "cashless society."

Under EFTS each consumer would have his own all-purpose money card, with a number and a foolproof means of identification such as a voiceprint or fingerprint. When he made a purchase, he would insert his card into a computer terminal device at the retailer's store. The device would hook up with a regional computer center and then the consumer's bank. With no cash or paper slips changing hands, the cost of the purchase would be deducted from his bank account automatically; if there were insufficient funds in the account, the customer could use an overdraft or "cash advance" privilege based on a pre-authorized line of credit. The amount of the purchase would automatically be credited to the retailer's account.

The primary purpose of a checkless society is to simplify the transactions of the nation's banking system, which is currently awash in paperwork. Some 30 billion checks are processed annually, and with the number expected to reach 45 billion by 1980, some experts fear the present system of transferring funds will

---

[31] Banks make money from credit cards in two ways: they get processing fees ("discounts") ranging from 1 to 6 per cent from merchants who allow customers to buy goods with the cards, and they obtain monthly finance charges—usually at an annual rate of about 18 per cent—from cardholders who choose not to pay their bills in full by the due date.

break down. But the implications of a cashless, checkless society are sweeping; so sweeping that in October 1974 Congress established a 26-member Commission on Electronic Fund Transfers to study the question.[32] EFTS could mean the end of cash crimes, from street robberies to political payoffs. All transactions would be traceable, recordable and revocable. Managing the economy to achieve stabilization or other social ends would be greatly simplified, since there would be no longer any mysterious, unwieldy money supply.

New problems would arise, however, including a new kind of criminal effort involving the manipulation of computers and data banks. The National Commission on Consumer Finance also feared that "the economies of scale inherent in the development of a massive electronic system for the exchange of funds and credit information lead naturally to oligopoly—that is, control of the industry by a few large credit grantors—with a consequent danger of restraint of competition and denial of its benefits to consumers seeking credit in the future." Even if the technology can be perfected, people would still have to be convinced that they would not lose their money or their privacy in such a system.

Importance of Education About Consumer Rights

Whether or not such a change is instituted, consumers will have to be increasingly well-educated to cope with the consumer credit economy. Counseling services such as those provided by the National Foundation for Consumer Credit are expanding, but they are primarily responsible for helping persons who are already in trouble. It is generally agreed that consumer education should begin much earlier, in high school or even elementary school. "We teach a kid how to drive a car," comments Mary Quinn-Callnan of the NFCC, "but we don't teach him how to pay for it."

Experience has shown that legislation is not enough to protect the interests of consumers; they must be taught their legal rights. Disclosure legislation is only as effective as the informed use consumers make of the disclosures. Consumer education, to be most beneficial, would be aimed not only at "middle America" but at consumers in the lower economic strata who presumably need it most. For them, the purchase of a car or color television set represents a special risk, and a special adventure. The prudent use of credit can broaden the range of choices available to consumers. As long as it continues to do so, it will remain an important part of the American economy and way of life.

[32] Members include the chairman of the Federal Reserve System, the Attorney General, the Comptroller of the Currency, the Postmaster General, the Secretary of the Treasury and the chairman of the Federal Trade Commission.

Selected Bibliography

Books

Chapman, John M., and Robert P. Shay, eds., *The Consumer Finance Industry: Its Costs and Regulation*, Columbia University Press, 1967.

Hendrickson, Robert A., *The Cashless Society*, Dodd, Mead & Co., 1972.

Homer, Sidney, *A History of Interest Rates*, Rutgers University Press, 1963.

Michelman, Irving S., *Consumer Finance: A Case History in American Business*, Frederick Fell Inc., 1966.

Russell, Thomas, *The Economics of Bank Credit Cards*, Praeger, 1975.

Articles

Chapman, Jane Roberts, "Women's Access to Credit," *Challenge*, January-February 1975.

"The Debt Economy," *Business Week*, Oct. 12, 1974, and selected issues.

"How to Shop for Credit," *Consumer Reports*, March 1975.

Maledon, Elick N. Jr., and Conway T. Rucks, "Bank Card Profitability: User Characteristics," *The Journal of Consumer Credit Management*, summer 1974.

" 'Easy Credit' Drives More and More Families to the Brink," *U.S. News & World Report*, July 15, 1974.

—"Soaring Debt in U.S.: Is It Getting Out of Hand?" Feb. 24, 1975.

Proxmire, William, "Consumer Credit: Privacy the Collateral," TRIAL (publication of the Association of Trial Lawyers of America), January-February 1975.

Reports and Studies

Editorial Research Reports, "Rights to Privacy," 1974 Vol. II, p. 785; "Banking Stability," 1974 Vol. II, p. 541.

National Commission on Consumer Finance, "Consumer Credit in the United States," December 1972.

Sub-Council on Credit and Related Terms of Sale of the National Business Council for Consumer Affairs, "Financing the American Consumer: A Business Report on Consumer Credit," November 1972.

PART 2
Business Woes

FUTURE OF UTILITIES

by

John Hamer

**1 9 7 5
Mar. 14**

FUTURE OF UTILITIES

T HE NATION'S PUBLIC UTILITIES, traditional pillars of the national economy, suddenly find themselves facing an uncertain future. It is a future fraught with hazard for the utility companies and for the public they serve. At stake may be the very survival of the utilities, at least in their present form. Without some fundamental changes, most experts believe, the nation's utilities will continue to be plagued by cash shortages, construction delays and stockholder unrest, while the general public will be confronted with ever-costlier utility bills, more frequent power blackouts or brownouts and other potential disruptions in vital services.

Of all the utilities, the electric power industry is the most troubled today, but it cannot be said to typify the nation's utilities. The electric industry is unique because it is the largest American industry in terms of total assets, the most capital-intensive industry in the entire economy, and the nation's largest fuel consumer.[1] Electric utilities require more investment every year than any other single industry—about 12 per cent of the annual total. They have kept pace with a demand for electricity that has doubled every 10 years since 1880, far faster than the overall growth in energy consumption.

An even-faster growth of electric power in the coming years is needed, according to the official blueprint for moving America closer to the goal of energy self-sufficiency. The Federal Power Commission envisions electric power accounting for 50 per cent of total energy use in 1980, in contrast to 25 per cent today. But a host of problems which have intensified in the first half of this decade casts doubt on the ability of the electric utilities to fulfill this expanding role. Inflation and recession have hit them harder than most other industries because of the utilities' vast size and enormous needs for fuel and capital. They have been hurt by high interest rates and a money squeeze, burdened by the quadrupling of foreign oil prices, hampered by shortages of labor and materials, and pressed by high costs of anti-pollution equipment.

[1] *A Time to Choose—America's Energy Future* (1974), final report of the Ford Foundation's Energy Policy Project, pp. 255, 256.

65

Moreover, the rate of growth in consumer demand for electricity fell abruptly last year. Americans used only 0.6 per cent more electricity than in 1973, far below the historic annual growth rate of 7 per cent.[2] Mild weather, reduced business activity, the Arab oil embargo, higher electricity rates, and energy conservation measures were all offered as explanations for the decrease, but the experts do not know if the growth rate will return to the traditional figure or remain at a lower level. This uncertainty is troubling to an industry that, years in advance, bases its expansion plans on anticipated future demand. "Looking ahead, it is hard to avoid a sense of despair about the utilities' future," Carol J. Loomis concluded in a recent analysis in *Fortune* magazine. "While some industries can look forward to relief when the recession ends, a return of rapid economic growth—without a damping of inflation—could actually make matters *worse* for the utilities."[3]

Consumer Complaints About Fast-Rising Rates

The electric utilities have responded to this critical situation in two ways: they have sought rate increases and they have cut back expansion plans. To raise rates, utilities must win the approval of regulatory commissions in most states *(see p. 72)*. Last year these commissions approved a total of $2.2 billion in rate increases, and early in 1975 they were being asked to approve more than $4 billion more. Nationwide, rates began rising in the late 1960s after many years of relative stability. From 1947 to 1967, electric rates went up only 12 per cent, while the general consumer price level increased by 50 per cent.

Since 1970, however, electric rates have gone up faster than the overall cost of living—three to four times faster in 1974, according to the Argus Research Corporation, a New York securities research firm. In the first half of 1974 alone, the 50 largest utilities increased the rates of industrial and commercial customers an average of 55.4 per cent, according to the National Utility Service Inc., a utility information group. Residential rates went up by an average of about 22 per cent in 1974, but in some metropolitan areas the average increase approached 40 per cent and some individual customers watched their bills more than double over a one-year period.

As a consequence, utility rates have become one of the most controversial issues of the mid-1970s. Consumers who reduced their consumption voluntarily to conserve energy are especially outraged to see their bills climbing higher. From New England

---

[2] "Project Independence Report," Federal Energy Administration, November 1974, p. 118.
[3] Carol J. Loomis, "For the Utilities, It's A Fight For Survival," *Fortune*, March 1975, p. 97.

to California, consumers have protested higher charges and have organized to fight their local utilities. Among the developments in various states:

> In *New York* last November, utility activists formed the Peoples Power Coalition of New York, which now has 60 member organizations and campaigns against rate increases.
>
> In *North Carolina,* a group called United Electric Consumers claims 78,000 members and has organized extensive letter-writing campaigns to influence utility regulators and state legislators.
>
> In *Virginia,* a group of utility customers formed the Virginia Citizens Consumer Council to protest a proposed rate increase and is raising $100,000 to finance its fight against rate increases.
>
> In *Florida,* Jacksonville citizens formed POWER, Inc.—People Outraged With Electric Rates—which claims 18,000 members in its fight to stop further rate increases.
>
> In *Maryland,* electricity consumers in one area turned off all of their lights and appliances for 15 minutes to protest a planned rate increase, and other customers are underpaying their bills in protest.
>
> In *California,* a group called Electricity and Gas for the People (E&GP) was formed to oppose rate increases by Pacific Gas and Electric (PG&E).
>
> In *Georgia,* the Georgia Power Project, a coalition of environmental, consumer, labor and low-income groups, successfully opposed a Georgia Power Company rate request and forced the utility to curtail its expansion program.

Similar organizations are springing up in many areas to protest rate increases, and they are clearly having an impact on state regulatory commissioners, who are either elected officials or political appointees. Utility commissions which traditionally granted rate increases almost automatically have become increasingly critical of utility rate requests. Last September, state utility regulators were called to Washington, D.C., where Secretary of the Treasury William B. Simon and top officials of the Federal Power Commission and the Federal Energy Administration urged them to grant rate increases to help the struggling utilities. But the National Association of Regulatory Commissioners instead called for an in-depth study of utility company management.

Objections to Controversial Fuel Adjustment Clause

One of the most controversial elements of the rate increase issue is the so-called fuel-adjustment clause, a device which allows utilities to pass on higher fuel costs automatically without public hearing or formal approval by the regulatory commissions. While fuel-adjustment clauses have long been on the books in at least 42 states, the practice is coming under

Increased Cost of Electricity for Residential Users

Metropolitan Area	1974 Over 1973	Metropolitan Area	1974 Over 1973
Atlanta	19.3%	Los Angeles	21.7%
Baltimore	23.7	Milwaukee	4.4
Boston	32.8	Minneapolis- St. Paul	15.1
Buffalo	14.4	New York	37.6
Chicago	9.1	Philadelphia	26.4
Cincinnati	10.1	Pittsburgh	16.7
Cleveland	29.1	St. Louis	7.2
Dallas	9.0	San Diego	25.4
Detroit	17.3	San Francisco-	
Honolulu	13.9	Oakland	11.7
Houston	7.5	Seattle	2.6
Kansas City	17.7	Washington, D.C.	25.1

Percentages are based on 1974 and 1973 averages, as compiled by the U.S. Bureau of Labor Statistics.

heavy fire in all of them. In the past, increases in fuel costs were negligible, but the quadrupling of foreign oil prices in 1973-74[4] and the big increase in coal costs suddenly began showing up on electricity bills with a startling effect on consumers. In New York City, about three-quarters of the increase in bills last year was due to the adjustment clause; in Boston, two-thirds; in Philadelphia, one-half; in San Francisco, almost 100 per cent, according to a study by *Consumer Reports* magazine, published by Consumers Union.[5]

The utilities argue that they have no control over increased fuel costs, are not making any profit on them, and cannot be expected to absorb the costs. Consumer groups object to the fuel-adjustment clause on several grounds. For one thing, they point out that many utilities now own coal mines or natural gas deposits and provide their own fuel. "With the fuel-adjustment clause in operation, a utility can buy fuel from itself at an artificially high price and pass that price on to the consumer," argued *Consumer Reports.* "In this way, though the utility may not increase its profit on the electricity it produces, it could make extra profit through a fuel subsidiary not subject to regulation."

Another objection to the device is that it removes any incentive utilities might have to negotiate for lower fuel prices from their suppliers, and thus contributes to high energy prices. The fuel-adjustment clause is being challenged on legal grounds in numerous places. Opponents question the right of states to grant monopoly powers to private electric utilities and then abrogate the regulatory authority. Among recent developments:

[4] See "Arab Oil Money," *E.R.R.*, 1974 Vol. I, pp. 365-380.
[5] "The Fuel-Adjustment Caper," *Consumer Reports*, November 1974, p. 837.

In *Vermont*, the state supreme court struck down the fuel-adjustment clause on the ground that it violated state laws requiring specific procedures in rate cases. The court required utilities to apply for fuel cost increases individually. These take effect automatically if the state utility commission fails to act within 24 days.

In *Florida*, at least four lawsuits have been filed seeking to prevent utilities from collecting fuel-adjustment costs, and the state public service commission now conducts monthly hearings on such cost increases.

In *North Carolina*, the state utility commission ordered three power companies to roll back fuel-adjustment charges by 25 per cent for two months, and bills have been introduced in the state legislature to ban the clause.

In *West Virginia*, the state public utilities commission found in a preliminary audit that the Appalachian Power Co. had overcharged its customers more than $2 million in 1974 through use of the clause, but the utility denied that it had done so.

In *Washington, D.C.*, the local public service commission found that Potomac Electric Power Co. had overcharged its customers by $1.8 million last year by including salaries, finance charges and building costs in the fuel-adjustment clause and by failing to include fuel cost refunds.

In *Maryland*, the public service commission ordered utilities, beginning in April, to stop including the cost of items other than fuel and its transportation in their fuel-adjustment charges.

Despite such actions against the fuel-adjustment clause, some utilities have pressed for authority to pass on automatically other increased costs, such as wages, taxes and pollution control. The Ford administration last fall expressed support for this effort, with Secretary Simon urging additional cost adjustments to help avoid "blackouts and brownouts and, worse, economic stagnation."

Troubled Financial Status of Big Electric Utilities

Many of these efforts to pass on more costs to the customer can be ascribed to the electric power industry's financial difficulty. "The most pressing financial problem in the energy sector pertains to public utilities," the Federal Energy Administration said in its Project Independence Report in November 1974.[6] "This is true in terms of its immediacy, its size and its impact on future energy supply." If electricity is to take on a larger share of U.S. energy consumption in the future, utilities must expand their capacity through a massive construction program. Ac-

---

[6] Project Independence was initiated in March 1974 to evaluate the nation's energy problems and provide a framework for developing a national energy policy.

Highest Rate Increases
by Major Electric Utilities, 1972-74*

Florida Power	99.8%	Massachusetts Electric	80.6%
Public Service of New Jersey	95.6	Baltimore Gas & Electric	79.8
		Jersey Central Power	70.0
Long Island Lighting	90.7	Virginia Electric and Power	67.9
Southern California Edison	90.4	Connecticut Power and Light	67.6
Consolidated Edison	87.9		
Philadelphia Electric	84.0	Potomac Electric Power	66.2

*Among the 35 largest utilities in the United States surveyed by National Utility Service Inc., based on charges to large commercial and industrial customers as of June 1972 and June 1974.

---

cording to some estimates, the industry must bring "on line"—into operation—at least as much generating capacity in the next decade as it has in the last decade, and perhaps more. The Project Independence Report estimated that $316 billion to $441 billion would be needed by the industry between 1975 and 1985.

Where is the money to come from? That question is haunting utility executives. In the past, when their financial requirements were much smaller, private utilities had little trouble raising funds. Now their enormous capital needs have begun to strain the money markets. The downward trend in the costs of building new power plants has ended; plants have reached the size where economies of scale no longer apply. Larger plants are no cheaper per kilowatt of generating capacity. Also, record high interest rates have been especially costly for the capital-intensive utility industry. So despite rate increases, cost increases have meant declining earnings for the utilities. According to the Federal Power Commission, the industry's operating expenses were up 37.4 per cent last year while revenues were up 31.6 per cent.

The slowdown in earnings has made investors wary of buying electric utility stocks and bonds. Consolidated Edison Co. of New York shocked Wall Street last April 23 by announcing it was suspending its annual dividend to stockholders. Wall Street had traditionally considered utility stocks "ideal for widows and orphans" because of their reliable earnings and safe dividend yields. Although Con Ed's situation was atypical, stockholders began unloading other utility stocks and the Dow Jones utility average abruptly dropped several points in a few days.

Since then, utility stocks have recovered somewhat as investors saw an opportunity to buy at what might be considered bargain prices. Last September, the Southern Company, a giant utility holding company, made the largest common stock offering ever by an electric utility—17.5 million shares at $9.50 a share, compared with a 1973 price of $17.25 a share. The offering was a great success and encouraged other utilities to announce similar offerings in an effort to raise money. But financial analysts warned that sales of inflated amounts of stock at depressed prices might create a new set of problems. A survey last fall, for example, showed that 24 electric utilities with an average book value of about $76 a share were trading their common stock at an average price of $42.69 a share, a 44 per cent discount.[7] Although this trend might attract investors for awhile, some experts feared that it would drive away buyers in the long run as existing stockholders saw their equity diluted by the selling of more and more shares at lower costs, thus reducing earnings per share and threatening new dividends even further.

Yet electric utilities have no choice but to finance future expansion through the sale of stocks and bonds, or by borrowing directly from financial institutions. In the past, most construction was financed internally through depreciation, tax deferrals and retained earnings; only 40 per cent of spending was financed externally. Utilities today depend on external sources for about 75 per cent of their funds for new plants and equipment. Many have had their bond ratings reduced on Wall Street, forcing them to pay higher interest rates to lure investors. "The situation will worsen as old bonds with low interest rates mature and are replaced by bonds with current higher interest rates," wrote Murray L. Weidenbaum, a utility economist at Washington University, St. Louis, in *Challenge* magazine.[8]

Widespread Cutbacks in Utility Construction Plans

Faced with such far-reaching financial difficulties, the nation's electric utilities have had to reduce their plans for expansion. From the present nationwide generating capacity of about 450,000 megawatts, the utilities had expected to expand by at least half again as much and perhaps to double their capacity in the next decade. But last year alone, they canceled or postponed construction plans by nearly half, reducing the capacity they were planning to build from 360,000 megawatts to 190,000 megawatts.[9] Most of the cutbacks have involved nuclear plants, which provide only about 7 per cent of the nation's electricity today but which the industry had hoped would provide as much as 25 to 50 per cent in the future.

---

[7] *The Wall Street Journal*, Oct. 17, 1974.

[8] Murray L. Weidenbaum, "The Future of the Electric Utilities," *Challenge*, January-February 1975, p. 47.

[9] *Business Week*, Jan. 20, 1975, p. 46.

In recent months, utilities have for economic reasons abandoned or delayed plans for more than half of some 180 new reactors they had intended to put in operation by 1985. Those canceled include a 2.3 million kilowatt (kw) plant by Consumer Power of Michigan; those postponed include an 825,000 kw plant by Florida Power, a 2.2 million kw plant by Georgia Power, a 1.14 million kw plant by Jersey Central Power & Light, a 2.3 million kw plant by Northeast Utilities of New England, and a 2.3 million kw plant by Public Service Electric & Gas of New Jersey.

National Economic Research Associates (NERA), a firm that has done extensive utility research, found in a survey that by December 1974 some 100 major utilities had cut their construction budgets through 1978 by $21 billion, almost one-fourth of their original budgets, representing 110,000 megawatts of nuclear generating capacity. As an alternative to nuclear plants, which take as long as 10 years to complete, many utilities have ordered gas turbines. Gas turbines are considerably cheaper and can be put into operation in about two to three years. But the low installation costs of turbines are offset by high fuel costs. They require either natural gas, of which supplies are dwindling, or light fuel oil, which is very expensive and also is used by residential customers.

Pressures on the Regulatory Structure

CAUGHT IN THE MIDDLE between outraged consumers and worried utilities are the regulatory agencies responsible for approving or rejecting rate-increase requests. Government regulation of the electric-power industry developed slowly. Thomas Alva Edison invented the electric light bulb in 1879, the first electric generator for arc lights was installed the next year in Rochester, N.Y., and Edison's famed Pearl Street station in downtown New York City—the world's first steam-operated electric generating plant—was opened in 1882. But it was not until 1907, in response to an outpouring of public concern over utility monopolies that the first three state regulatory agencies were established in Wisconsin, New York and Georgia.

Private, investor-owned electric utilities are regulated today in 46 states. In Texas, South Dakota and Minnesota, regulation is by local government agencies, while Nebraska has no private utilities. Only about a third of the states regulate publicly owned utilities. Although regulation varies among the states, most utility commissions have broad powers to ensure that utilities

U.S. Electric Industry

More than 75 per cent of U.S. electricity is produced by about 300 private, investor-owned utility companies which dominate the industry. The remainder is supplied by public power systems. These include some 2,075 municipal or regional systems which provide about 15 per cent of electricity, and about 960 rural electric cooperatives which supply less than 10 per cent.

The federal government generates about 12 per cent of the nation's electricity through five large agencies which sell power wholesale to both private and public utilities: the Tennessee Valley Authority, the Bonneville Power Administration, the Southwestern Power Administration, the Southeastern Power Administration and the Bureau of Reclamation. Many public power systems also purchase electricity wholesale from investor-owned companies.

Only about 33 per cent of the nation's electricity is used by the residential sector. The largest portion, 40 per cent, is consumed by industry. Twenty-three per cent is used by the commercial sector, including stores, offices and schools. The remaining 4 per cent is used for miscellaneous purposes. Electricity can be produced from oil, natural gas, coal, hydro (water) power, nuclear power, or from solar, wind, geothermal, tidal or other new energy sources if they become available.

Most electricity in this country is produced by fossil fuels burned in power plants to heat water and produce steam, which drives turbines to turn electric generators. Coal is the primary fossil fuel used for power generation today, followed by natural gas and oil. Hydroelectric power provides about 15 per cent of the electricity and nuclear power about 7 per cent.

provide satisfactory service at reasonable rates. Some commissions have authority over utility accounting methods, financing arrangements and expansion programs. About 30 commissions have jurisdiction over the siting of power plants and transmission lines.

"Under present inflationary conditions, the fate of investor-owned utilities is, as never before, in the hands of the regulators," utility analyst Fergus J. McDiarmid wrote in *Public Utilities Fortnightly*.[10] In many cases the regulators are small-town lawyers, independent businessmen or local politicians who may be unprepared for the sudden increase in pressure on their jobs. According to a study by the Edison Electric Institute, a New York trade group representing investor-owned utilities, 175 rate increase cases were pending before state regulatory commissions in January 1975, compared with only 59 at the end of 1970.

---

[10] "Public Utilities on the Ropes," *Public Utilities Fortnightly*, Sept. 12, 1974, p. 35.

While utility companies spare no expense in hiring lawyers, accountants and economists to prepare their rate-increase applications, most state commissions lack sufficient budgets or adequate staffs to analyze the evidence thoroughly. Two critics of the regulatory process wrote in *The Progressive*: "So on the one side at the rate hearing is the company, with several hundred pages of testimony, exhibits and computer printouts, along with the best attorneys, rate engineers, and consultants money can buy. On the other side, representing the beleaguered ratepayer is—usually—no one at all. The lowly ratepayers simply cannot compete in such a situation."[11] A few state commissions have appointed "public counsels" to represent the consumer in rate cases, but they are seldom a match for the powerful and well-paid forces of the utility companies.

However, pressures on regulatory commissions from the customers' side have increased greatly in recent months. Consumers and environmentalists sometimes have joined together to form advocacy groups. Many of them have been inspired or aided by the Environmental Action Foundation's Utility Project, established in 1972 to help local citizens study and act on electric utility issues. The organization now is in contact with many groups around the country that are opposing higher rates and fuel-adjustment clauses, challenging nuclear power plants and other new facilities, working for rate structure reform or trying to set up public power systems. The project also acts as a clearinghouse for information and prepares its own reports on utility issues. One of its most influential publications is a 100-page report, "How To Challenge Your Local Electric Utility: A Citizen's Guide to the Power Industry," by Richard Morgan and Sandra Jerabek. It has sold more than 12,000 copies since its publication in March 1974.

Complex Process of Determining Utility Rates

Regulatory commissions set rates allowing the utilities a fixed percentage of profit on their total invested capital, or *rate base*. Because the *rate of return* is fixed, utilities can increase profits only by increasing the rate base. Thus companies have little incentive to keep construction and equipment costs down, critics contend, because the more they spend the more they make. Regulatory commissions use a formula to determine how much money utilities may collect from their customers. The first element in the formula is *cost of service*, which usually includes fuel costs, maintenance, salaries, advertising and public relations expenses, taxes and *depreciation*. Depreciation, as an

---

[11] Ed Meyers and John Musial, "The Electric Scandals of '75," *The Progressive*, March 1975, p. 25.

accounting method, permits a company to recover the costs of its plant and equipment over a period of years.

The rate of return—historically around 6 per cent but in recent years often 8 to 10 per cent—is applied to the rate base to arrive at *net operating income.* The rate base and cost of service are calculated over a one-year period called the *test year,* most often the last complete calendar year before the rate increase is requested. Once all of these factors have been determined, the net operating income is added to the cost of service to arrive at *gross revenue.* After this figure is determined, the company must set customer rates calculated to bring in that amount of revenue.

Critics of the private utilities contend that the actual functioning of the system allows utilities to earn higher rates of return than they are theoretically allowed by regulatory commissions. According to the Environmental Action Foundation's Utility Project, a Senate subcommittee survey in 1967 found that the average rate of return then authorized by state utility commissions was 6.14 per cent, but Federal Power Commission figures indicated the actual rate of return that year was 7.3 per cent. In an extreme example, Montana Power Company was supposedly earning 5.33 per cent on its rate base, but FPC statistics showed it was actually getting 11.37 per cent.

Questions Over Bookkeeping and Taxing Methods

Some differences of this kind can be attributed to the methods of assigning value to various items included in the rate base. Most commissions use a *depreciated original cost* rate base, which takes the original cost of equipment and subtracts the amount of depreciation over the years. Depreciation is taken on the *straight-line* method, which means that if a power plant is supposed to last for 25 years, 1/25 of its value is subtracted each year and charged to the rate base as an operating expense. But some utilities have argued successfully that the depreciated original cost method is unfair because the replacement costs of new equipment are so high. About a third of the state commissions thus consider both the original cost and the *reproduction cost new* of utility property to arrive at a *fair value* for the rate base.

In addition, there are numerous tax advantages available to utilities. They may use *accelerated depreciation* to depreciate property more rapidly than it actually wears out. This reduces the tax liability during the early years of an asset's life while increasing it in later years, thus delaying tax payments. They may use the federal investment tax credit to deduct 4 per cent of new investment expenses; however, this is less than the 7 per cent allowed many other businesses. Most utilities use *normalized ac-*

counting procedures, which means they keep two sets of books—one for the state regulatory commission and the other for the Internal Revenue Service. The books shown to the state may include the amount of taxes that would be paid without the use of accelerated depreciation or investment tax credits. The difference between this amount and that which is actually paid in taxes in a given year is placed in an *accumulated tax deferrals* account. Until funds from the account are paid to taxes years later, they continue to provide the utility with extra money.

Some new tax advantages have been added in recent years, including the *interest during construction* allowance, which lets utilities claim interest expenses on capital tied up in building costs. Many states allow utilities to include *construction work in progress* in the rate base. In that way, companies with large construction programs can as much as double their rate bases. Moreover, some commissions allow utilities to base their rate increase applications on a *future test year* rather than actual expenses during a previous year. "This arrangement opens up the regulatory process to conjecture and makes it nearly impossible for consumers to question expense figures," Morgan and Jerabek wrote. Another controversy arises over *interim rate increases* granted before hearings are completed on rate requests, since the hearing process can take months or even years. Although refunds must be awarded if the permanent increase is not granted, critics contend that the practice tends to make interim increases permanent and circumvent the public hearing process.

Federal Agency Control of Wholesale Pricing

Although most of the rate decisions directly concerning electric-power users are made by state commissions, the Federal Power Commission has had a significant role in utility regulation since 1935. That year the Public Utility Holding Act extended its jurisdiction to the interstate transmission of electricity and gave it authority to set rates for the wholesale purchase of electric power. Until then, from the time of the FPC's founding in 1920, the commission had been limited to the licensing of non-federal hydroelectric projects.[12]

By setting rates for all wholesale and interstate sales of electric power, the commission exerts a strong influence on what the public ultimately must pay at retail for the electricity it uses. The FPC also regulates the accounting standards that most state commissions and utilities follow, and periodically audits books, as do the state commissions. The FPC shares some authority over utility securities, mergers, and acquisitions with the Securities and Exchange Commission.

---

[12] See "Power Policies of the Roosevelt Administration," *E.R.R.*, 1933 Vol. II, pp. 331-335.

Conflicting Approaches to Utility Reform

THE FORD administration and Congress are considering a variety of ways to aid the utility industry. The federal government is worried about the unemployment and recessionary impact of cutbacks in electric-power construction plans. Cutbacks already announced represent $21 billion worth of construction. In addition, they represent potential electric-power generation sufficient to reduce the American oil demand by 3.3 million barrels a day. That saving could cut the current level of U.S. oil imports in half; it represents four times more oil than is imported from the Middle East.

In his 1975 State of the Union address on Jan. 15, President Ford set out a detailed energy plan to be known as the "Energy Independence Act." As submitted to Congress on Jan. 31, the legislation included several proposals to help the utilities. To place the utilities on a sounder financial basis, Ford would limit state regulatory commission action on proposed rate increases to five months, eliminate bans on fuel-adjustment clauses, allow utilities to include the costs of construction and pollution control in their rate bases, and allow them to charge customers less for use of electricity during off-peak hours. He also requested an increase in the investment tax credit for utilities from the present 4 per cent to a temporary level of 13 per cent.

In addition, Ford asked Congress to extend for two years, to mid-1977, the Federal Energy Administration's authority to require power plants to convert to coal from oil or natural gas, and to require new power plants to have coal-burning capacity. He proposed delaying some deadlines for compliance with certain air pollution standards. Ford also asked for FEA authority to oversee development of a national plan for siting new energy facilities. Finally, he proposed the deregulation of natural gas *(see box, p. 200)*.

The Environmental Action Foundation, together with the Consumers Federation of America and the Public Interest Research Group, charged that the plan "would make a mockery of the process of utility regulation" and "amounts to an unwarranted subsidy for the power industry from American consumers and taxpayers, and a reward for the industry's mismanagement of the nation's electric system." The groups said that the proposal would cause a 20 per cent increase in electricity rates and enable most utilities to escape payment of federal income taxes.

Natural Gas Regulation

Natural gas, which provides one-third of America's total energy requirements, is the nation's cheapest and cleanest fuel. But natural gas supplies are dwindling, according to most experts, and the Federal Power Commission—which regulates natural gas—has urged mandatory conservation measures and allocations to high priority uses.

The FPC for 20 years has set the price at the wellhead for all natural gas sold in interstate markets. In the past when supplies seemed ample, prices were set at low levels to encourage consumption. Demand for natural gas doubled between 1957 and 1972, but the rate of exploration and development of new gas fields declined.

The Ford administration has proposed deregulation of natural gas to allow prices to rise and encourage exploration. Critics of deregulation argue that without FPC controls, consumers will be left at the mercy of the major oil companies, the leading producers of natural gas. Deregulation would create windfall profits, critics say, without assuring production of more gas.

Congress has rejected deregulation proposals in recent years and there appears to be considerable opposition in the 94th Congress. But the gap between supply and demand for natural gas is a chronic problem in the United States, and one that could cause serious disruptions in the nation's economic system.

An additional problem is lack of reliable data. Previous federal estimates have said that the nation has some 2,000 trillion cubic feet of natural gas reserves, but the National Academy of Sciences' National Research Council in February 1975 estimated that the reserves could be as small as 600 trillion cubic feet.

The administration also has asked that utilities be allowed to treat preferred stock dividends as interest payments, which would make them tax-deductible. The Securities and Exchange Commission already has stopped requiring utilities to seek competitive bids from underwriters on new stock issues. This action has seemed to boost utility stock offerings.

Herman Roseman, president of National Economic Research Associates, believes that an average 12 per cent rate increase would give the utilities enough cash flow to keep their construction programs on schedule, if followed by "realistic" increases in the future. Raising the specter of industrial shutdowns due to lack of electricity, T. Justin Moore Jr., president of Virginia Electric and Power Co., has said: "It doesn't do any good to have low electricity bills if you have to pay them out of your unemployment check."[13]

---

[13] Quoted in *Business Week*, Jan. 20, 1975, p. 48.

William G. Rosenberg, chairman of the Michigan Public Service Commission, advocates a program of federally guaranteed bonds and federal purchases of preferred stock to help utilities raise funds for vital construction. This would "assure the availability of the required capital on a dependable basis at a reasonable cost," Rosenberg wrote in *The Wall Street Journal,* Jan. 8, 1975. He proposed that the Federal Power Commission establish an insurance fund and guarantee debt service payments on qualifying debt securities issued by investor-owned utilities. "A nation that guarantees financing of electrical service to its rural citizens through the Rural Electrification Administration has an equal obligation to assure service to the urban areas through the investor-owned utilities."

Reaction to the Rosenberg proposal has been decidedly mixed. Most utility executives have deep misgivings about direct federal aid or control. Other opponents object that a federal credit program would do little to increase the total flow of savings or investment, and would merely enlarge the share of funds going to the utility sector of the economy.

Calls for Rate Reform to Encourage Conservation

One proposal on which there seems to be wide agreement is that electric rates should be restructured to discourage increased use. Traditionally the charge per kilowatt-hour decreased as consumption increased, because in the past, utility costs declined with volume. But today, adding capacity to a power system raises rather than lowers the per kilowatt-hour cost. Now comes the idea of "inverting" the rate structure so that large users—primarily industrial customers—pay more as consumption goes up, or at least pay the same "flat" rate as everyone else.

Another suggestion is for higher prices during "peak load" periods—times of the day or year when electricity consumption is greatest, such as just before mealtime when electric ranges are in heavy use, or during summer months when air-conditioning use goes up. The problem is that utilities must have the capacity to meet maximum peak demand—often using old and inefficient equipment at those times—but their facilities sit idle during off-peak periods. Some companies, including Virginia Electric and Power Co. and Long Island Lighting Co., already impose higher rates during summer months to try to discourage consumption. But time-of-day rates would require new electric meters costing as much as $100 apiece. Despite that drawback, Wisconsin and New York public service commissions are studying the feasibility of time-of-day pricing. Some European countries have been using the method for many years.

To help low-income customers, reformers have proposed a "lifeline" rate to guarantee a certain amount of electricity to the poor at minimal cost. Their aim is also to prevent disruption of service for non-payment of bills in hardship cases. Several states have already adopted the lifeline concept.

Prospect of Public Takeover of Private Utilities

Of all the challenges to private utilities today, none is more far-reaching than the suggestion that the government take over investor-owned utility companies. Theodore E. Maynard, president of National Utility Service Inc., a New York consulting firm, considers electricity so basic a commodity "that the profit motive should be taken out." Alex Radin, director of the American Public Power Association, agrees: "Consumers are probably better off under government-controlled utilities. We pay no taxes, no dividends, no high-powered salaries to executives."[14] Among other observers, the author of *Fortune's* study mused: "Oddly enough, the prospect of takeovers might not be all bad news for the companies' stockholders. In today's conditions, a takeover of a utility's properties might be the best thing that could happen to its owners. Which suggests how deep the industry's problems go."

However, public power systems are not without problems. Morgan and Jerabek of the Utility Project warn that "some publicly owned companies exhibit the same disdain toward citizens as do most investor-owned utilities." Nonetheless, in the 25 per cent of the nation served by public systems, the rates tend to be considerably lower. The main reason for the lower rates is that many public systems purchase electricity from federal agencies such as the Tennessee Valley Authority and the Bureau of Reclamation, which have access to cheap hydropower and can sell at bargain prices.

Another factor is that public power systems pay no local or federal taxes, and issue tax-exempt bonds to finance new facilities. Moreover, rural electric cooperatives borrow money from the government at low interest rates. "The cost of these taxpayer subsidies should be considered when the benefits of public power are being analyzed," Morgan and Jerabek wrote. "Many environmentalists oppose these subsidies which tend to lower the cost of electricity in public power systems." However, the Utility Project endorses the concept of public power, saying that it removes the profit motive, makes the utilities more responsive to environmental concerns and gives the public a role in the decision-making process.

Although municipally owned systems and rural cooperatives are the most common forms of public power systems, another

---

[14] Both quoted in *Business Week*, Jan. 20, 1975, p. 54.

Telephone Utility Problems

The nation's telephone utilities, while not as hard-pressed as electric utilities, also have sought rate increases to cover rising costs in recent years. The Federal Communications Commission, which regulates interstate telephone rates, announced on Feb. 27 that it would approve a $365 million annual rate increase to the American Telephone & Telegraph Co. (AT&T) long-distance telephone service. The company had asked for a $717 million increase, contending that higher rates were necessary to help meet increased costs and boost earnings to attract capital for expansion programs.

In addition, some telephone companies that are regulated by state public service commissions have sought rate increases for local and intrastate service. A 15-cent charge for calls from coin-operated telephones has been approved in the states of North Carolina and Washington, and in the District of Columbia. Other phone companies now are charging residential customers a fee for directory-assistance calls, most of which involve numbers readily available in the telephone book. The companies say they need increased revenues to cover escalating expenditures for new plant and equipment. According to *Business Week* magazine, the industry's annual expenditures more than doubled between 1966 and 1974, from $6 billion to $14 billion a year.

model is the Public Utility District (PUD). These districts exist primarily in the state of Washington. Non-profit PUDs operate independently of other government agencies, buy most of their power at a low cost from the Bonneville Power Administration and turn part of their receipts back to local general revenue funds. A similar system nationwide has been suggested by James Ridgeway and Bettina Conner of the Institute for Policy Studies.[15]

Another possibility is a national power grid. A federal agency would be responsible for major generation and transmission facilities and for construction of new capacity, while allowing the existing utility systems to distribute the power locally. Sen. Lee Metcalf (D Mont.) has introduced legislation to establish a National Grid Corporation, and the plan has been endorsed by the National Rural Electric Cooperative Association. In Massachusetts, citizen groups are pushing for a statewide referendum on their plan to set up a state power authority to take over major generation and transmission facilities. A major obstacle to state takeover is the lack of funds that plagues most state governments. Whatever is done to solve the utility problems, it is clear that action is needed soon.

[15] "The Elements," published by the Institute for Policy Studies' Transnational Institute in affiliation with the Movement for Peoples Power, January 1975.

Selected Bibliography

Books

Berlin, Edward, Charles J. Cicchetti and William J. Gillen, *Perspective on Power*, Ballinger Publishing Co., 1974.

Energy Policy Project, Ford Foundation, *A Time To Choose: America's Energy Future*, Ballinger Publishing Co., 1974.

Farris, Martin T. and Roy J. Sampson, *Public Utilities: Regulation, Management and Ownership*, Houghton-Mifflin, 1973.

Metcalf, Lee and Vic Reinemer, *Overcharge*, David McKay Co., 1967.

Articles

Electrical World, selected issues.

Karen, Robert, "Our Obsolete Utility Rates," *The Nation*, March 30, 1974.

Loomis, Carol J., "For the Utilities, It's A Fight for Survival," *Fortune*, March 1975.

Love, Sam, "Reddy Kilowatt's Dark Hour," *The Progressive*, December 1974.

Novick, Sheldon, "Report Card on Nuclear Power," *Environment*, December 1974.

Public Utilities Fortnightly, selected issues.

Radin, Alex, "Utilities and Inflation," *Public Power*, September-October 1974.

Ridgeway, James and Bettina Conner, "New Energy," *The Elements*, January 1975.

"The Fuel-Adjustment Caper," *Consumer Reports*, November 1974.

"Those Shocking Electric Bills And the Complaints They Bring," *U.S. News & World Report*, Feb. 24, 1975.

"Utilities: Weak Point in the Energy Future," *Business Week*, Jan. 20, 1975.

Weidenbaum, Murray L., "The Future of the Electric Utilities," *Challenge*, January-February 1975.

"Will the Government Bail Out the Utilities?" *Business Week*, Sept. 14, 1974.

Studies and Reports

Editorial Research Reports, "New Energy Sources," 1973 Vol. I, p. 185; "Electric Power Problems," 1969 Vol. II, p. 937; "Electric Power Supply and Regulation," 1965 Vol. II, p. 939.

Federal Energy Administration, "Project Independence Report," November 1974.

Interior and Insular Affairs Committee, U.S. Senate, "Electric Utility Policy Issues," 1974.

Morgan, Richard and Sandra Jerabek, "How to Challenge Your Local Electric Utility: A Citizen's Guide to the Power Industry," Environmental Action Foundation's Utility Project, March 1974.

RAILROAD REORGANIZATION

by

David Boorstin

N o. 9
Mar. 7

RAILROAD REORGANIZATION

T HIS IS THE YEAR for the United States to come to terms with its railroad problems. After years of indecision about a proper fate for ailing and failing railroads in the Northeast and Midwest regions, a preliminary official blueprint now exists. After additional hearings, evaluations and possible amendments, Congress will have to either reject the plan by autumn or else acquiesce in its acceptance.

The preliminary plan as drawn up by the federal government would replace the outworn rail transportation system which now serves 17 eastern and midwestern states[1] and half of the country's population. Seven bankrupt railroads *(See p. 89)*, the mammoth Penn Central Among them, are included in the Preliminary System Plan for restructuring the rail system in that region. The plan was released on Feb. 26 by the United States Railway Association (USRA), an agency created by the Regional Rail Reorganization Act of 1973 to reorganize the bankrupt lines into "an economically viable system capable of providing adequate and efficient rail service...."

USRA's board of directors[2] said in the Preliminary System' Plan that the region should be served by three major rail systems. The act established the Consolidated Rail Corporation, or ConRail, as a federally aided for-profit corporation to acquire and operate those parts of the bankrupt lines to be included in the new system. In addition, the plan would provide for the expansion of the solvent Chessie System (a combination of the old Chesapeake & Ohio, Baltimore & Ohio and other property) and the Norfolk & Western Railway. ConRail, the board said, "is not intended to be a composite of bankrupt carriers, but a revitalized, restructured railroad serving the same territory now served by the bankrupt carriers."

---

[1] Connecticut, Delaware, Indiana, Illinois, Maine, Maryland, Massachusetts, Michigan, New Hampshire, New Jersey, New York, Ohio, Pennsylvania, Rhode Island, Vermont, Virginia and West Virginia, plus the District of Columbia.

[2] Arthur D. Lewis, a former investment banker and airline executive, is chairman of the 11-member board which includes the Secretary of Transportation, the Secretary of the Treasury, the chairman of the Interstate Commerce Commission, and seven non-government members who were recommended by organizations representing state and local government, organized labor, the financial community and shippers.

To achieve this goal, USRA proposed substantial rehabilitation and pruning of the existing rail system in the 17 states. It said that upgrading tracks, facilities and equipment could cost $5 billion over the next 15 years and that rehabilitating 110,000 freight cars and acquiring 20,000 new freight cars and 800 engines could cost an additional $2.3 billion. With the elimination of 6,200 miles of "light density" branch lines, as proposed, USRA calculated that ConRail could operate the remaining 15,000-mile system at a profit after the third year of operations.[3] Many analysts, however, questioned whether the rail system could ever operate in the black. Their doubts were underscored Feb. 26, when the Chicago, Rock Island & Pacific Railroad warned of a shutdown unless federal help was forthcoming.

Arthur D. Lewis, chairman of USRA, cautioned in the Preliminary System Plan that the association "can only plan a system and recommend methods of financial assistance." He said "others will have to share in the creation of an environment favorable to an economically viable rail system for the nation." He spoke of the need for the country's recovery from the current recession, for changes to be made within the railroad industry, for greater labor productivity[4] and for a lessening of government regulation. "Shippers and passengers will have to bear a larger share of the costs of providing rail services," Lewis added.

Implementing such changes will not be easy in the face of opposition from some solvent carriers, competing sectors of the transportation industry, and those customers, taxpayers and legislators who are reluctant to supply the funds. If the reorganization effort fails, however, the alternative is likely to be nationalization, which Lewis called "a solution no more desirable now than it has been in the past," and one which could generate even stronger opposition.

Problems Confronting Preliminary System Plan

In addition to setting up USRA, the Regional Rail Reorganization Act of 1973 established a Rail Services Planning Office within the Interstate Commerce Commission (ICC) to evaluate plans developed by USRA and to study the views of state and local officials, shippers and manufacturers and others who have an interest in rail services. Under a timetable set by law, the Office will hold hearings on the Preliminary System Plan and by

---

[3] According to USRA projections, ConRail would move from a $91.4 million loss in its first year of operation to a modest profit in 1978 and, by 1985, achieve a pre-tax profit of $381.7 million—a level of profitability about on par with the rest of the industry.

[4] The association said it expected no substantial reduction in railroad employees under the plan, although there will be a shift in some types of employment as the emphasis is put on rebuilding and rehabilitating rail facilities. If ConRail achieves profitability, an increase in railroad employment can be expected within a decade, according to USRA.

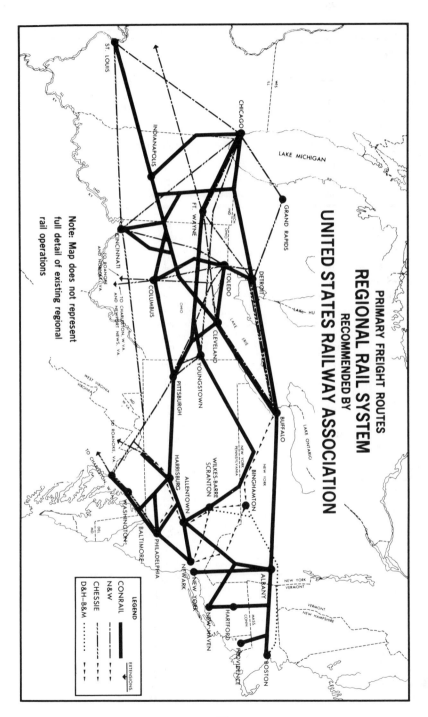

PRIMARY FREIGHT ROUTES
REGIONAL RAIL SYSTEM
RECOMMENDED BY
UNITED STATES RAILWAY ASSOCIATION

Note: Map does not represent
full detail of existing regional
rail operations

LEGEND
CONRAIL
N&W
CHESSIE
D&H–B&M

EXTENSIONS

87

April 27 will provide USRA with its evaluation; by July 26 the association will submit a Final System Plan to Congress. Unless specifically rejected by Congress by Sept. 24, the plan will be put into effect for ConRail to begin operations in January 1976.

Congressional rejection or acquiescence will depend largely on how well the final plan is seen as fulfilling the statutory goals set for a new rail system: one which will be economically viable and will meet the needs of the Northeast and Midwest. Moreover, the new system must be created and operated at the lowest possible cost to taxpayers, and it must take into consideration environmental standards, competition, energy conservation and community welfare in areas affected by changes in service. "Some of these goals seem to be in competition with one another," the USRA commented in its first annual report to Congress and the President, "thus a successful...reorganization will require a sensitive balancing of interests with the understanding that each goal may have to be compromised to some degree." The key issue, however, is whether the new rail system can be made profitable—not highly profitable, but enough so to be successfully reorganized and sustained by private capital:

> Anything less may lead to the collapse of ConRail, dissipation of its assets, direct governmental responsibility for its deficits and its continued existence in some form as a nationalized company. The implication that this possibility has for the ultimate nationalization of the whole rail industry is significant.[5]

Questioning of System's Financing and Competition

The continuing financial plight of the Penn Central Railroad has made financial viability especially important in the eyes of many, but it also has led to skepticism that ConRail will be able to fare much better. Since it went into bankruptcy in June 1970, the Penn Central has lost some $1.3 billion—a record deficit for American enterprise. In an appearance before the House Committee on Interstate and Foreign Commerce, Feb. 5, 1975, the railroad's trustees said that they would have to start closing down operations as of Feb. 18 because of the company's inability to meet its payroll. Soon afterward, Congress considered emergency funding, and on Feb. 26—the same day the Preliminary System Plan was released—a bill authorizing $347 million[6] in federal aid for the Penn Central and other struggling lines was approved and sent to the White House. In the meantime the trustees postponed the shutdown.

---

[5] United States Railway Association, *Annual Report, June 30, 1974, With A Supplemental Report Through October, 1974*, pp. 43-44.

[6] Of the total, $150 million is for loans for capital improvements and $197 million is for direct grants to pay operating expenses. The latter amount is still subject to congressional appropriation in a separate bill.

Bankrupt Lines for Reorganization

Following are the seven bankrupt lines included in the restructuring, their line mileage and their operating revenues in 1972:

Penn Central	19,459 miles	$1.8 billion
Reading	1,128 miles	$111 million
Lehigh Valley	972 miles	$51 million
Central of New Jersey	324 miles	$42 million
Ann Arbor	299 miles	$11 million
Lehigh & Hudson River	86 miles	$2 million
Erie Lackawana*	2,932 miles	$264 million

* Not until Jan. 9, 1975, when the Preliminary System Plan was in the final stages of preparation, did the Erie Lackawanna's trustees ask for it to be included in the reorganization process under the act. Thus the USRA largely excluded it from the plan, except to propose that its main line be purchased or rented by the Norfolk & Western railroad.

Fears were expressed, however, that even this sum might be insufficient to keep the Penn Central running until ConRail takes over its operations. The Rail Reorganization Act had provided $85 million in federal grants to keep the bankrupt roads running until reorganization took effect. The Penn Central had already exhausted its $62.5 million share, in addition to $16.4 million worth of federal disaster loans following Hurricane Agnes in 1972 and $100 million worth of Treasury-guaranteed loans to meet expenses in 1970-72. Thus, despite hopes for a "private sector" solution for ConRail, *Business Week* magazine said "The almost inescapable conclusion is that...rail service in the Northeast will be maintained only through permanent support from federal, state, or local government agencies."[7]

Another critical factor in congressional consideration is the competitive effects of ConRail on other railroads and other forms of transportation. USRA "recognizes that excessive competition between railroads at times has led to greater costs, reduced or erratic service and higher rates for shippers, but elimination of rail-rail competition in key markets is an unacceptable policy under the mandate of the act."[8] The preliminary plan is designed to provide "a pervasive level of competition with at least two large carrier systems competing in every large market throughout the region." Talks are under way with both the Chessie System and the Norfolk & Western to see whether they are interested in taking over the proposed routes.

[7] "Recession Derails the Penn Central," *Business Week*, Jan. 13, 1975, p. 36.
[8] United States Railway Association, *Preliminary System Plan*, p. 107.

There are doubts that an agreement can be reached: the chairman of the Norfolk & Western has said he opposes the plan.

State and Local Fears of Track Abandonment

Of all the issues involved in railroad restructuring, none has been more controversial than the future of branch lines. The goal of economic self-sufficiency, which demanded that ConRail should not be burdened with operating unprofitable services, conflicts with the goals of fulfilling the region's rail needs and minimizing the adverse effects of reorganization. Attention was focused on the problem more than a year before the Preliminary System Plan was released, when the Department of Transportation made public a report on "Rail Service in the Midwest and Northeast Region," Feb. 1, 1974. The DOT Report, as it was known, was the first step in the restructuring process under the Rail Reorganization Act, and it contained the department's conclusions and recommendations with regard to all rail services—solvent and bankrupt—in the region. The report said 15,-575 miles of the 61,000 miles of track it studied were "potentially excess."

The Rail Services Planning Office held hearings on the report which raised serious questions about many aspects of track abandonment. There was dispute over the data selected and the methodology used to determine excess lines. Some unprofitable lines, it was pointed out, are crucial as "feeder" lines to profitable parts of the system. Even after financially unviable track has been identified, it is difficult to measure the socially destructive effects that could follow abandonment. The basic economic assumptions behind abandonment of branch lines were also attacked. Pennsylvania Gov. Milton J. Shapp, an outspoken critic, contended that "Few railroaders believe that massive abandonment of branch lines will effect important savings, while community and business leaders know that rail abandonment can cause substantial economic hardship."[9]

USRA tested the assumption that profitability was inexorably tied to the elimination of uneconomic service and concluded that branch lines are indeed a significant part of the railroad problem. After making a line-by-line analysis of 9,600 miles of "light density" lines of the bankrupt railroads, the agency recommended that 3,400 be retained as part of ConRail's 15,000 mile system; it said this system will be able to handle 95.5 per cent of the freight handled by the bankrupt roads in 1973. The other 6,200 miles of lines will be analyzed further to determine

---

[9] From Shapp's counter-proposal to the Railroad Reorganization Act, "A United States Rail Trust Fund," 1974, p. 32. He would make all of the nation's railroads eligible for capital-improvement grants, totaling $12 billion to $13 billion over a six-year period, to be financed by a 5 per cent surcharge on rail freight revenues.

whether they should be (1) acquired by a solvent railroad, (2) included in ConRail, or (3) be made available for some form of public subsidy as provided by the act.

Under Title IV of the act, $90 million is authorized for each of the next two years to subsidize the continuation of local rail services if a state is willing to match every $70 of federal spending for this purpose with $30 of its own funds. If the $90 million is matched fully by the states, nearly $130 million will be available annually for the subsidy program; USRA has calculated that this would be enough to continue in operation all of the branch lines not included in ConRail. Even so, there are potential problems. To become eligible for the funds, states will have to draw up their own rail plans and specify which unprofitable lines they are willing to help subsidize. More money will be needed after the two years are up. Furthermore, the funds provided under the act subsidize operating expenses only; funds to rehabilitate run-down branch lines have not been provided.

Track abandonment is an emotional issue expected to occupy much of the hearings on the Preliminary System Plan. Even before the plan was officially released, some officials were protesting it. Governor Shapp called the plan a "disaster" that could lead to nationalization. New York State Transportation Commissioner Raymond T. Schuler objected: "Shippers and consumers in New York State simply cannot accept a plan which could lop some 975 miles from their state's rail-freight network and which threatens mainline and branch-line customers alike with less frequent, more costly service."[10]

In its report on the Rail Reorganization Act, the House Interstate and Foreign Commerce Committee stated that the act "recognized the need for safeguards for small areas, to be able to continue essential service which is not economical for the carrier. This was recognized as a social cost to be borne by the government."[11] Yet measuring the ultimate size of that cost, and determining who should pay it, will not be easy.

Development of U.S. Railway Policy

DURING THEIR first quarter-century of existence, beginning in 1826,[12] American railroads were nearly all clustered in New

---

[10] Quoted in *The New York Times*, Feb. 27, 1975.

[11] House Report 93-620, pp. 28-29.

[12] A four-mile length of track was opened that year to haul granite in horse-drawn cars from quarries to the docks at Quincy, Mass. The first locomotive appeared in America three years later.

York and New England and served predominantly local needs. Until 1850, the Baltimore & Ohio was the only long-haul railroad in the nation. This condition changed quickly, however, once the government began to conceive of the railroad as a means of nation-building. To open up the West and bind the country together, Congress instituted a series of land-grant programs beginning in 1850 and ending with the Pacific Railroad Act of 1862.

Through land grants, loans and tax concessions, federal and state and local governments fostered a rapid growth of railroads. The federal government gave railroad companies 6.8 per cent of the nation's total land area, and it is estimated that federal financial aid to the railroads amounted to $175 million during this period.[13] This then-enormous sum was matched by state and local governments. At the end of the Civil War, there were 35,085 miles of track in the United States. Within the next decade this figure had more than doubled to 74,096 miles, and by 1887 it had doubled again.[14]

Most of the granting acts, about 70 in all, gave the railroads a right-of-way 200 feet wide plus sections of land 20 miles deep in the form of a checkerboard pattern along the right-of-way. In all, as much as 49 million acres of the federal domain were given to the railroads in this manner. The railroads, in turn, were expected to sell the land to homesteaders, thus accomplishing a dual purpose—raising money to build the railroad and settling the land. George L. Banker wrote that "From their inception, the railroads helped to corrupt federal, state and local governments, charged exorbitant freight rates, and divided the country into a monopolistic system of rate pools."[15] Banker, writing in 1973, estimated that in the western United States, the railroads still owned 24 million acres—an area almost as large as Pennsylvania.

Railroad Excesses and Development of Regulation

The years before and after the Civil War—a time of robber barons and freebooting—left the railroads with a reputation from which they still suffer. They hired immigrants, including Chinese coolies, paid them starvation wages and sometimes worked them literally to death. Protesters and strikers were clubbed back to work. Since there was as yet little or no competition between the lines, they charged exorbitant freight rates. When competitive lines did develop, the companies entered into

---

[13] First figure cited by John F. Stover, *American Railroads* (1961), p. 88, and the second by Carter Goodrich, *Government Promotion of American Canals and Railroads, 1800-1890* (1960), pp. 267-71.

[14] Figures cited by Ann F. Freidlander in *The Dilemma of Freight Transport Regulation* (1969), a publication of the Brookings Institution, p. 9.

[15] George L. Banker, "The Kingdoms of the Railroads," *The Nation*, March 12, 1973.

pooling arrangements and gentlemen's agreements to protect their monopolies, or else into ruinous rate wars.

The attitude of 19th century railway tycoons was expressed by William Henry Vanderbilt, son of Commodore Cornelius Vanderbilt who had built the New York Central. Questioned by two reporters in his private railway car on Oct. 8, 1882, the younger Vanderbilt said: "The railroads are not run for the benefit of the dear public. That cry is all nonsense. They are built for men who invest their money and expect to get a fair percentage in return." When a reporter asked him whether the trains were not supposed to be run for the commonweal, Vanderbilt made his famous reply: "The public be damned." He later denied using profanity.

"The railroads are not run for the benefit of the dear public.... The public be damned."

The financier J. P. Morgan moved at this time of rate wars to keep peace between major lines—for a price. His role as an arbitrator of railway disputes dated from 1885 when he effected a peace agreement between the Pennsylvania and the New York Central. Congress, meanwhile, was unwilling or unable to curtail the abuses and excesses of the railways. It is estimated that more than 150 bills and resolutions seeking to control rates were introduced in Congress between 1868 and 1886, but all were blocked by the powerful railway lobby. Finally, public pressure prevailed and Congress in 1887 passed the Act to Regulate Commerce, setting up the first federal regulatory agency, the Interstate Commerce Commission.[16]

Regulation was hampered for years by litigation and inadequacy in the powers of the regulatory authority. Strengthening amendments added to the original law in 1906, 1910 and 1920 brought a gradual increase in the powers and prestige of the Icc. Under the Transportation Act of 1920, the commission finally gained full rate-making authority. Its regulatory powers, originally confined to rail carriers, were extended in 1935 to interstate motor carriers and in 1940 to coastal and inland water carriers.

---

[16] Historians disagree whether the railroads supported or opposed the creation of the Icc. While the railroads feared government control, they were also trying to end a long period of rate wars.

When the ICC was established, the railroads monopolized both short- and long-haul freight and passenger traffic. That situation, modified to a significant extent only by the building of interurban streetcar lines in the early 1900s, continued through World War I. The rail carriers began to encounter competition from private automobiles and from intercity bus lines and trucking companies in the 1920s, and from domestic airlines after 1938. Gasoline rationing and transportation demands during World War II restored heavy passenger and freight loads to the rails in the first half of the 1940s, but thereafter all semblance of the old rail transportation monopoly vanished. Its demise led railroad companies to complain bitterly of over-regulation and to seek wider freedom to battle with their competition for a bigger share of the transportation market.

Federal Operation of Railways in World War I

Railroad nationalization is seen by some as a threatening eventuality to be avoided at all costs. Yet government operation of the railroads would not be a new experience for the United States. For 26 months—from January 1918 through February 1920—the country's railroads were operated by the United States Railroad Administration, headed by Secretary of the Treasury William G. McAdoo. This was done to achieve enough railway efficiency to meet the demands generated in World War I; President Wilson took possession the day after Christmas 1917, under authority of a provision of the Army Appropriation Act of 1916.[17]

In one sense, the experiment was a success. The entire rail system became far more efficient than at any time previously. Accumulation of traffic at terminals had reached a peak in May 1917 when there was a shortage of 164,000 freight cars. At war's end in November 1918, the shortage had been cut below 15,000 cars, despite an enormous increase of freight traffic in the intervening period. The reduction, however, was effected in part through such costly expedients as moving empty boxcars the width of the country.

In his *War History of American Railroads,* Walker D. Hines, who succeeded McAdoo as director general in January 1919, computed the average annual cost of operating the railroads under federal control at $4.4 billion, or 83 per cent more than the average annual operating cost of $2.4 billion during a three-year test period before the war. Hines pointed out, however, that the rise of operating costs was not out of line with increases in costs in private industry during the war period.

---

[17] See "Government Ownership of Railroads," *E.R.R.*, 1938 Vol. I, pp. 237-240, and "Railroad Subsidies," *E.R.R.*, 1961 Vol. II, pp. 837-853.

While public opinion favored return of the railroads to private ownership after the war, organized labor and various farm organizations campaigned unsuccessfully for continued public operation and for transfer of ownership to the federal government. The question of nationalization came to the fore again during the Depression Thirties, a time when 36 Class I railroads (those with annual revenues of $5 million or more) and many smaller lines went into bankruptcy. In his first report as federal coordinator of transportation,[18] Joseph B. Eastman asserted in 1934: "When an industry becomes so public in character that such intimate regulation of its affairs becomes necessary, in strict logic it would seem that it should cease to masquerade as a private industry and the government should assume complete responsibility, financial and otherwise." Eastman did not call for outright nationalization, however, because "the country is not now financially in a condition to stand the strain of an acquisition of these great properties."

Quarter Century of Railroad Decline; Public Aid

Railroads emerged from World War II with more business than they had the capacity to handle, and they enjoyed comparatively good times until the business recession of 1949. After that, railroad fortunes declined drastically as their competitive situation deteriorated. Revenue passenger miles declined 80 per cent from 1947 to 1973 despite explosive growth in passenger travel generally, and railroad growth lagged far behind that of the economy in general:

> In 1947 the railroads carried nearly-two-thirds of the intercity freight; by 1973 that share had dropped to 39 per cent. During the same period, when the gross national product grew approximately 170 per cent (after adjusting for inflation) and while industrial production grew 219 per cent, total U.S. rail revenue ton miles grew only 30 per cent while ton miles carried in the Eastern District...actually declined 17 per cent.[19]

There was no single cause for this decline. It was the result of many complex factors: improved technology of rival forms of transportation; massive public support for road, water and air traffic; basic changes in underlying market conditions as industry shifted locations, and as heavy industry and agriculture gave way to a service-oriented, high-technology economy, especially in the Northeast; the inability of the railroads to adjust to market changes, since their facilities were

---

[18] The federal coordinator was appointed under the Emergency Transportation Act of 1933 to work for the elimination of unnecessary rail services and to promote a financial reorganization of the bankrupt carriers. The position was eliminated when the act expired on June 16, 1936.

[19] *Preliminary System Plan*, p. 2. The Eastern District embraces substantially the area to which the plan applies.

fixed in place; management and labor problems; and the legacy of a harsh regulatory climate.[20]

Congressional action to aid the ailing railroads was generally sketchy and involved no new legislation of major consequence until the Transportation Act of 1958 authorized the ICC to operate a $500 million program of loan guarantees for the purchase of new equipment. The measure was intended to improve the competitive position of railroads by also authorizing the ICC to allow them to discontinue some services and charge less for others. The Railroad Loans Extension Act of 1961 extended for two years the loan guarantee authority of the ICC.

Despite this assistance, railroads called for more government help in 1961 to avert a "major crisis." Their plight was further publicized that year by an ICC report on reorganization of the bankrupt New York, New Haven and Hartford Railroad, stating that the line could not "emerge from reorganization proceedings as a privately owned enterprise unless it is the recipient of substantial government assistance." The ICC proposed a $52 million bail-out of the railroad but Congress refused.

Passage of Rail Reorganization Act of 1973

The financial collapse of the Penn Central Transportation Company, the largest passenger and freight carrier in the country, triggered a series of events which eventually brought the railroad problems to the floor of Congress.[21] The Penn Central filed bankruptcy proceedings in federal district court in Philadelphia on June 21, 1970, and for the next three years struggled vainly to reorganize under Section 77 of the Federal Bankruptcy Act.

During the period seven more railroads declared bankruptcy: the Ann Arbor, the Boston & Maine, the Central of New Jersey, the Erie Lackawanna, the Lehigh Valley, the Lehigh and Hudson River, and the Reading. These, too, had difficulties reorganizing for continued operations under Section 77; but like the Penn Central, they were too essential to the regional and national economies to be allowed to cease running. Together, the eight railroads moved more than 45 per cent of the freight in the eastern region. Although the seven are tiny by comparison with the mammoth Penn Central, their failures intensified the problem. Federal, state and local governments, labor leaders, consumers, shippers and the industry itself recognized that it had reached crisis proportions.

---

[20] See Congressional Quarterly's *Congress and the Nation*, Vol. I (1965), p. 553.

[21] For background, see *The Wreck of the Penn Central* (1971), by Joseph R. Daughen and Peter Binzen. See also "Railroad Nationalization," *E.R.R.*, 1973 Vol. I, pp. 461-62.

Reorganization and the Courts

The collapse of the Penn Central, the most stupendous business failure in American history, has produced such a legal tangle that two periodicals—with subscription prices of $2,400 and $600 a year—are published solely to help stockholders, lawyers and creditors keep up with the case. It is "the biggest piece of litigation that ever will exist," according to Newell Blair, publisher of the *Corporate Reorganization Reporter*. "The magnitude of it is just beyond the brain to comprehend." Estimates of the total legal expenses in the case run up to a million dollars a month.

Soon after the Rail Reorganization Act became law, it was challenged by creditors of the bankrupt railroad, mainly insurance companies and banks. They challenged the constitutionality of the act on the ground that stock in ConRail, which they are to receive in exchange for current rail properties, may prove to be as worthless as that of the Penn Central is now. A federal court in Philadelphia held parts of the act unconstitutional, which threatened to halt reorganization.

On Dec. 16, 1974, the Supreme Court reversed that decision and upheld the constitutionality of the act by a 7-2 vote, ruling that the railroads involved would not be giving up their property in the reorganization without adequate compensation. The Supreme Court's decision was satisfactory to most of the parties concerned, for while the reorganization could continue, creditors could file suit against the federal government in the U.S. Court of Claims to retrieve any losses—which could amount to billions of dollars.

On Feb. 1, 1973, Penn Central trustees called for a federal solution to the financial problems which plagued the debt-ridden company. They requested $600 million in interim federal aid over a four-year period and asked for the relaxation of regulatory controls by the ICC. The trustees maintained that they could restore the Penn Central to financial health if they were allowed to lay off 5,700 of its 80,000 employees and abandon unprofitable lines. They estimated that only 11,000 miles out of 19,864 were profitable. The Nixon administration rejected their request Feb. 7, and the next day, when Penn Central was scheduled to begin its plan to eliminate one of the two brakemen carried on most trains, 28,000 members of the United Transportation Union struck the Penn Central.

In the face of massive public concern at the potential effects—General Motors warned it would have to shut down in a matter of days—Congress on Feb. 8 cleared emergency legislation to end the strike, and directed the Secretary of Transportation to submit to Congress within 45 days a plan for preserving rail service in the Northeast. On March 26 the Department of Transportation presented its rail plan calling for the creation of a new for-profit railroad corporation to operate a sharply reduced Northeast rail system with virtually no federal assistance.

Then on July 12, in a sudden about-face, Secretary of Transportation Claude S. Brinegar asked for an $85 million appropriation for direct grants to bankrupt lines to keep them operating until the new corporation could take over. The reversal came just nine days after Judge John J. Fullam, presiding over the Penn Central bankruptcy case, authorized the trustees to file with the ICC their plan to stop all service on Oct. 31, and later to liquidate the entire system. Finally, on Oct. 1, the ICC asked Fullam not to close down the system, but instead to wait for congressional action.

"It may take a generation of lawsuits to determine whether the taxpayers or some other interests got the best of the bargain."

This came in the form of a bill initially drafted by officials of the profitable Union Pacific railroad, who feared that the liquidation of the Penn Central would cut their own railroad's access to the Atlantic seaboard and hinder their ability to raise funds in the future. The solution, like the problem, was unprecedented and complex. Observers disagreed on whether the bill was likely to save the railroads as a private enterprise operation or constituted a first step toward railroad nationalization.

It did, however, allow for the special interests of labor (by providing generous allowances to employees who lost their jobs under the reorganization); shippers (by providing federal loans and grants to communities to keep in operation routes which the new corporation decided to abandon); creditors (by making them eligible for federally backed loan guarantees if the courts ruled that they had been paid too little for the assets the new corporation took over); and Amtrak *(see p. 99)* and solvent railroads in the region (by making federal loan guarantees available to healthy railroads in the Northeast and to railroads on the verge of bankruptcy).

"The whole thing," Joseph Albright wrote in *The New York Times Magazine,* "sounds like a gigantic experiment in Special Interest Socialism." While the alternative—allowing the Penn Central's creditors to shut down the railroad and auction off the pieces—might well have been disastrous, "It may take a generation of lawsuits to determine whether the taxpayers or some other interests got the best of the bargain."[22] The legislation authorized $558.5 million in appropriations plus $1.5 billion in loan guarantees to reorganize the bankrupt railroads. Signing the bill into law, President Nixon said that "some of these expenditures are higher than I believe they should be."

It now appears clear that the total cost for reorganization will be three to five times higher than was envisaged by Congress, with peak federal involvement forecast at $3 billion in the mid-1980s. And there are fears that by the time the Penn Central's creditors have litigated all of the claims allowed them by a Supreme Court ruling in 1974 *(see box, p. 97),* the cost could run to billions more. Another source of concern is that the legislation provided a precedent for temporary nationalization that could apply to other large, ailing companies. The new railroad system, ConRail, will be government-controlled for at least 20 years, and perhaps forever; the reorganization act stipulates that its board of directors must be controlled by government appointees as long as at least half of ConRail's outstanding loans are government assisted.

Concern for Viability of U.S. Railroads

THE FUTURE of rail passenger service, as well as freight, will be affected by the Usra's plan. In the busy Northeast Corridor from Boston to Washington, the association recommended that freight trains be rerouted to parallel lines and that track and equipment be upgraded to permit the development of reliable high-speed passenger service. Sixteen short-to-medium distance corridors in other densely populated areas in the region were also designated for new or improved passenger service.[23]

Most of the region's intercity rail passenger traffic is handled by Amtrak, the National Railroad Passenger Corporation, which assumed responsibility for most of the nation's intercity passenger trains on May 1, 1971. A nationalized system in everything but name, Amtrak was created under the Rail Passenger Service Act of 1970 to save passenger service and soon found itself handling an unexpected upsurge in traffic.

Amtrak has been plagued with problems. A report in 1973 by the General Accounting Office (Gao) described many of its

---

[22] "The Penn Central: A Hell of a Way to Run a Government," *The New York Times Magazine,* Nov. 3, 1974, p. 17.

[23] The most significant of these would be between Cincinnati and Detroit; Cleveland and Pittsburgh; Chicago and Cleveland; and Washington and Pittsburgh. These would be served by intermediate speed trains (80 mph), beginning operation in three to five years, after the tracks have been rehabilitated.

deficiencies. Although a follow-up review by a subcommittee of the House Committee on Interstate and Foreign Commerce in June 1974 found that "the condition of Amtrak trains has improved considerably in the...18 months since GAO conducted its review," the investigation disclosed "a number of significant unsatisfactory conditions on all trains seriously detracting from the performance, reliability and comfort to which passengers are entitled." These included uncomfortably bumpy rides, broken heating and air-conditioning, dirty and broken windows, and "innumerable instances" of porters, waiters and attendants being discourteous and unhelpful.

Passengers on an Amtrak train out of Tampa, Fla., last summer became so irate when the failure of its air conditioning led to 100 degree temperatures that upon arriving in Savannah, Ga., an hour behind schedule, they threatened to set fire to one of the cars. "The incident raised new questions about the ability of Amtrak management to cope with the rising demands for space on board crowded trains...and for its relations with the nation's private railroad industry—which must bear the responsibility for sharp increases in accidents and train delays during recent months," observed William H. Jones of *The Washington Post*.[24]

As the oil shortage drew passengers out of automobiles and sent air fares soaring, Americans began to rediscover trains. There were many predictions of a rail-travel renaissance. In 1974 Amtrak carried 18.5 million passengers, a 10 per cent increase over 1973. But Amtrak's myriad problems led to doubts about its ability to cope with the increase. Lateness became chronic: "Amtrak's on-time records look so bad they can make you throw up," said Anthony Haswell of the National Association of Railroad Passengers, a consumer group.[25]

Recriminations Between Amtrak and Railroads

The basic problem is that Amtrak does not own the tracks or haul or repair its own trains: that is done by 14 private railroads on a contract basis. This divided responsibility has led to indifferent service and buck-passing between the railroads and Amtrak. The railroads contend that the corporation's decrepit equipment is at fault. Most of Amtrak's equipment—some 2,112 cars and 453 locomotives—is World War II vintage and 30 per cent of it is likely to be in the shop at any one time.[26] According

---

[24] Aug. 25, 1974.

[25] Quoted by Rush Loving Jr. in *Fortune*, May 1974, p. 273.

[26] Some 347 new cars and 51 diesel and electric locomotives are on order. However, even new equipment can be unreliable, as was shown one week in January 1975 when 50 Metroliners, which ordinarily travel under their own power between New York and Washington, had to be pulled by 35- to 40-year-old Penn Central locomotives. The Metroliners, America's fastest trains, were incapacitated by snowy weather.

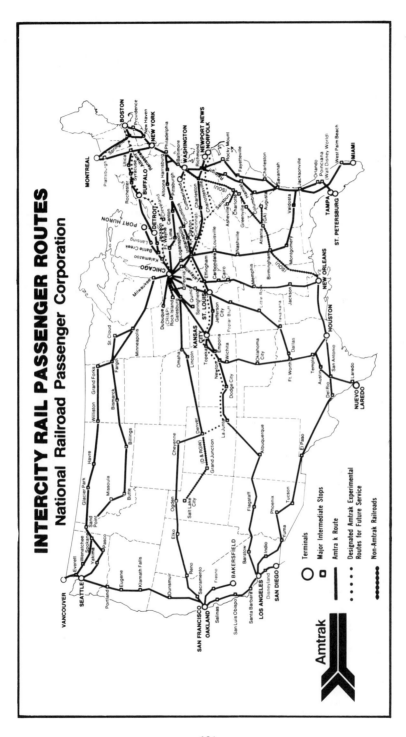

INTERCITY RAIL PASSENGER ROUTES
National Railroad Passenger Corporation

Amtrak

○ Terminals
□ Major Intermediate Stops
━━━ Amtrak Route
••••• Designated Amtrak Experimental Routes for Future Service
●●●●● Non-Amtrak Railroads

to Amtrak, new incentive-penalty contracts with 10 of its member railroads "finally broke the back" of problems with late trains and unreliable schedules on its 24,315 mile system. In addition, Amtrak during 1974 added 3,674 employees to its payroll—bringing the total to over 8,000—as it moved toward more control of its own service operations.

Amtrak's troubles were seen by many as being primarily a failure of management. In particular, Roger Lewis, as chairman and president of the corporation, was criticized for not getting the best performance out of it. Lewis and many of the senior managers came from the airlines, and they were accused of taking a disdainful attitude toward the railroads. On Jan. 29, 1975, Paul H. Reistrup replaced Lewis as president of Amtrak.[27] Reistrup had been senior vice president of Illinois Central Gulf Railroad and won national attention with his innovative attempts to upgrade the Baltimore & Ohio Railroad in the mid-1960s. "I've never seen an operation that had a larger catalog of problems," Reistrup said upon taking control.[28] "We are looking at a situation where expenses are twice as high as revenues."

Amtrak's operating deficit rose from $158.6 million in calendar year 1973 to $272.7 million in 1974. The deficit estimate for the fiscal year beginning in mid-1975 is $350 million. In his budget request for $360 million for Amtrak operations, $10 million above the deficit estimate, President Ford said: "These funds, while adequate to continue and improve existing service, are intended to be a maximum federal commitment within which Amtrak must operate." However, the corporation had earlier submitted to the executive branch and to Congress an ambitious five-year financial plan, calling for expenditures for additional new equipment and the investment of $1.2 billion over six years to substantially improve track, roadbed and signal systems of 12 separate short- and medium-distance "corridor" routes.

Physical Deterioration and Concern Over Safety

Massive amounts of money will be necessary in the next few years if the Northeast rail system is to be salvaged, much less upgraded. Out of the Penn Central's 38,500 miles of track, some 8,500 are currently under "slow orders"—the track is so dilapidated that the maximum allowable speed is 10 miles per hour.[29] Jervis Langdon Jr., president of Penn Central, insists

---

[27] Lewis remains on the board of directors.

[28] Quoted in *The Wall Street Journal*, Jan. 30, 1975.

[29] There are six grades of track, according to the Federal Railroad Administration, and each is suitable for a different speed. A track is put under slow orders when it is below the standard for its class. During the summer of 1974, FRA ordered one Penn Central line—the Chicago-Louisville run—closed down because 67 of its 419 miles did not even meet the minimum standards for 10 mile-per-hour operation.

Rail Passenger Service Here and Abroad

Most travelers agree that passenger rail service in the United States compares unfavorably with that in the rest of the world's developed nations. A report in June 1974 on Amtrak operations by the House Committee on Interstate and Foreign Commerce observed: "By comparison to Japanese and European passenger trains, American trains are extremely slow and antiquated and run much less frequently." Paul J. C. Friedlander wrote in *The Washington Post*, Jan. 26, 1975, that "Europe continues dominant in world railroading.... [T]he trains, their schedules, service and reliability...make an American question how they can do it when we cannot."

One answer is that, in the words of *The Economist* of London, "Most European governments seem quite content to go on pouring cash into loss-making railways." The magazine reported Feb. 1, 1975, that British Rail's deficit in the coming year is estimated at $700 million. Holland, with the nearest thing to a profitable railway in Europe, makes up an annual operating deficit of about $175 million. Another reason for the success of railways overseas, some observers maintain, is state ownership of rail networks.

that "The condition of the property, while not improved, is not deteriorating as fast as it once was."[30] The railroad spent some $300 million on maintenance in 1974 but, because of inflationary rises in the cost of track materials, it was unable to provide as much maintenance as in the previous year. To stop deterioration entirely, the Penn Central would have to spend 50 per cent more than it is able to now.

Since the early 1950s, chronic cash shortages forced the railroads to defer much of their spending for maintenance. What they are now trying to overcome is almost two decades of neglect. A team of six engineers from some of the nation's profitable railways reported to the Department of Transportation last summer that it would take $4.6 billion in expenditures by 1980 to restore the Penn Central system. More than $2 billion of that would have to come from outside sources.

The money would be used to buy new rails, restore roadbeds and railroad ties, and fix up train yards, some of which are in a "deplorable state," according to the report. Because massive government grants or loan guarantees will be needed to rehabilitate rail lines, the USRA plan recommends consideration of separate ownership and financing of tracks, yards, and rights-of-way. A Consolidated Facilities Corporation (ConFac) would acquire these assets, rehabilitate them with funds provided or

---

[30] Quoted in *Business Week*, Sept. 28, 1974, p. 66.

guaranteed by the government, and then make them available to ConRail.

In the meantime, the Penn Central must continue operations though it can barely keep running without spending huge sums to rebuild its facilities. Section 215 of the Railroad Reorganization Act made available $150 million in loans to improve track and equipment; $146 million has gone to the Penn Central. The money was delayed for some time by legal problems: first, the only tracks it could be spent on to improve were those that USRA administrators had determined would be in the final system plan; and second, there was the "double-buy" problem. The USRA was unwilling to spend money fixing up tracks that would become more valuable and so would cost the USRA more when the time came to buy them from the creditors.

"...Hazardous materials are passing hourly over poor tracks in the most heavily populated regions of the country, literally exposing millions of people to danger...."

These problems have been overcome, but there is still a lack of sufficient funds. The Penn Central is sitting on a potential gold mine of scrap metal in the form of old railroad cars, but the creditors will not allow this asset to be turned into cash to be reinvested in the Penn Central estate, since that estate is eroding day by day. Because the courts prevent the railroad from selling assets to put the money into the property, the bankrupt company cannot legally make capital improvements. So the Penn Central is compelled to improvise and do patchwork repairs, which in the long run will prove to be far more expensive.

The railroad has to turn away business "at the rate of $150,000 a day," according to one trustee, for lack of locomotives, cars, and track to run over at efficient speeds. But the cost of slow and dangerous track is great in other ways as well. Train accidents in the United States reached a 16-year high of 9,698 in 1973 and in 1974 were running at an even greater rate.[31] Forty per cent in 1973 were attributed to track defects. The Federal Railroad Administration (FRA) has only 38 track inspectors for some 300,000 miles of track, and 76 motive-power and equipment inspectors for more than 1.7 million freight cars and 25,000 locomotives.

---

[31] During the first nine months of 1974, 7,868 accidents were recorded—up from 7,015 in the same period of 1973.

The potential seriousness of these accidents is magnified by the hazardous nature of rail cargoes such as chlorine, liquid propane gas, hydrochloric acid, ammonia, sulfuric acid and crude cyanide. Congress recognized the danger when it passed the Hazardous Materials Transportation Control Act of 1970. But a report by the House Interstate and Foreign Commerce Committee in 1974 maintained that "the potential for disaster has mushroomed since that time because of the industry maintenance program. Unfortunately, nothing in the testimony before the committee, nor in staff research, gives any indication that conditions will become better before they get worse."[32]

The committee report pointed out that the deteriorating Penn Central, the nation's leading carrier of chemicals, serves 59 military installations and operates in the most urbanized parts of the country, where the majority of the nation's manufacturing plants are located. "Thus hazardous materials are passing hourly over poor tracks in the most heavily populated region of the country, literally exposing millions of people to potential danger without their even knowing the danger exists," the report said.

If trains are to fulfill the promises being made for them in a nation growing conscious of energy and environmental concerns, they must be made not only safe but efficient and appealing to passengers and shippers. A report endorsed and authorized by the Association of American Railroads, an industry group, said in 1970 that "Because railroading...may well be more adaptable to automated controls and computer technology than any other transport mode, there is great potential for fruitful research. At present, however the United States lags far behind other nations in promoting technical research in such areas as railroad dynamics, high-speed freight trains, higher loads and cybernetics."[33]

The same money problems that have led to deferred maintenance and the deterioration of large sections of America's rail system have also precluded such research. A successful reorganization of America's railroads is viewed as an important step toward future changes that will enable trains to realize their full potential.

---

[32] House Report 93-1083 on a bill (HR 15223) authorizing funds in fiscal 1975 and tightening the enforcement provisions of the Federal Railroad Safety Act and the Hazardous Materials Transportation Control Act of 1970. See *Congressional Quarterly Weekly Report*, June 15, 1974, pp. 1562-63. See also "Hazardous Cargoes," *E.R.R.*, 1974 Vol. II, pp. 747-764.

[33] America's Sound Transportation Review Organization, "The American Railroad Industry: A Prospectus," 1970, p. 41.

Selected Bibliography

Books

Binzen, Peter, and Joseph R. Daughen, *The Wreck of the Penn Central*, 1971.
Congressional Quarterly Almanac, 1973.
Freidlander, Ann F., *The Dilemma of Freight Transport Regulation*, Brookings Institution, 1969.
Stover, John F., *American Railroads*, 1961.

Articles

Albright, Joseph, "The Penn Central: A Hell of a Way to Run a Government," *The New York Times Magazine*, Nov. 3, 1974.
Banner, Paul H., "The Energy Situation—A Rail Viewpoint," *Transportation Journal*, spring 1974.
Business Week, selected issues.
Harbeson, Robert W., "Some Policy Implications of Northeastern Railroad Problems," *Transportation Journal*, fall 1974.
Locomotive Engineer (official weekly of the Brotherhood of Locomotive Engineers), selected issues.
Loving, Rush Jr., "Amtrak Is About to Miss the Train," *Fortune*, May 1974.
Meyer, John R., and Alexander L. Morton, "A Better Way to Run the Railroads," *Harvard Business Review*, July-August 1974.
Samuelson, Robert J., "Why Stories Make It: A Tale of Two Loans," *Columbia Journalism Review*, March-April, 1974.
"What's To Blame For Amtrak's Woes," *U.S. News & World Report*, Dec. 30, 1974.

Studies and Reports

America's Sound Transportation Review Organization, "The American Railroad Industry: A Prospectus," June 30, 1970.
Editorial Research Reports, "Railroad Nationalization," 1973 Vol. I, p. 459; "Railroad Subsidies," 1961 Vol. II, p. 837; "Hazardous Cargoes," 1974 Vol. II, p. 745.
National Railroad Passenger Corporation, "1974 Amtrak Annual Report," Feb. 15, 1975.
Rail Services Planning Office, Interstate Commerce Commission, "Evaluation of the Secretary of Transportation's Rail Services Report," May 2, 1974.
Shapp, Milton J., "A United States Rail Trust Fund," 1974.
Special Subcommittee On Investigations of the Committee On Interstate and Foreign Commerce of the House of Representatives, "Review of Amtrak Operations," June 1974.
United States Railway Association, *Annual Report June 30, 1974, With A Supplemental Report Through October, 1974*.
—*Preliminary System Plan for Restructuring Railroads in the Northeast and Midwest Region*, Feb. 26, 1975.

Book PUBLISHING

by

Mary Costello

1 9 7 5
May 9

BOOK PUBLISHING

B OOK PUBLISHING, like many other businesses, faces "a year of crisis" in 1975.[1] Publishers, caught in the current inflation-recession and hard hit by high interest rates and printing, binding, shipping and storage costs, have been forced to raise the price of their books, cut back on the number published, lay off employees and reduce payments to authors. But higher book prices have led to lower sales and large inventories of unsold books which must be remaindered—discounted to a fraction of their original price—stored or destroyed.

Industry optimists suggest that the gloom may be exaggerated. They point out that during the depression 1930s, many Americans gave up their more expensive leisure pursuits and turned to reading. Book sales remained relatively strong during that period. Others, however, are convinced that the book-buying public will turn to television or free lending libraries if the economy does not improve or if the price of books, up 10 per cent in the past year, does not come down. They also note that there was no inflation after the 1929 crash and that book prices remained relatively low in the 1930s.

The present economic downturn has hurt the two major book categories, *trade* (books sold primarily through stores) and *education* (books used in the schools and reference books). Particularly hard hit has been general hardcover fiction for adults and juveniles. Non-fiction hardcover sales, except for a few Watergate-related books and other best-sellers, have also shown some decline. Individual buyers are resisting these high-priced books or waiting until they are published in paperback, and libraries have been forced to cut back on their annual purchases. Library purchases have been running at about $448 million a year, according to trade sources.

Even the fastest-growing categories—textbooks and paperbacks—have been meeting sales resistance. A decline in college enrollment growth, higher textbook prices and the increasing use of paperbacks and audio-visual material have cut into the profits of college textbook publishers. Elementary and secon-

---

[1] Title of a seminar sponsored by the Association of American Publishers (AAP) in New York on Jan. 29, 1975. AAP is a group of more than 260 publishing firms and the major voice in book publishing in the United States.

dary schools ("el-hi") publishers have been hit by cutbacks in government spending for education. The paperback market, which has shown the most spectacular growth over the last ten years, slackened somewhat in 1974.

This situation has encouraged the nation's 1,205 book publishers[2] to cut back on the more than 40,000 titles published in 1974, to use more effectively the almost $100 million spent for advertising, to improve market research techniques, to find less expensive printing and binding methods, and to reduce the number of salaried workers. Staff layoffs, the most publicized of which was the firing of almost 200 employees at Macmillan last October, have led to considerable interest and activity among publishing employees in unionizing.

The drive for unionization, virtually unheard of in this low-paying, high-prestige field a few years ago,[3] highlights an important change in book publishing over the last several decades. Nearly all of the privately owned houses, headed by "gentlemen publishers," have been bought up by huge conglomerates. These mergers include the RCA's purchase of Random House, Alfred A. Knopf and Pantheon; the Columbia Broadcasting System's acquisition of Holt, Rinehart and Winston; Time Inc.'s absorption of Little, Brown; ITT's purchase of Bobbs-Merrill; Simon & Schuster's merger with Gulf & Western; and the Italian conglomerate IFI International's acquisition of Bantam Books. Joan Lappin, a senior analyst for the Dreyfus Corp., asserts that publishing companies that are publicly owned "cannot be run as gentlemanly undertakings, but must be profit-making enterprises."[4]

Cost-Cutting Retrenchments in Trade Publishing

Macmillan announced that it would reduce the number of trade books it publishes this year to 135, down from 200 last year, cutting general-interest adult and juvenile titles by 50 per cent. Random House will cut its list from 222 to 196 while Charles Scribner's announced reductions of 30 per cent and Viking Press of 20 percent. This retrenchment will mean that many fledgling authors, particularly novelists, will have a much harder time getting published and that fewer scholarly works will be accepted.

Publishers also want to reduce advances and royalty payments to authors, which have risen substantially in recent years. The advance is a payment to the author before the book is published. Royalties are a percentage of the list price on all

---

[2] According to 1972 Census Bureau figures, up from 1,022 in 1967.

[3] Starting salaries for college graduates today in publishing usually range from $125 to $135 a week.

[4] Quoted in *Publishers Weekly*, Nov. 25, 1974, p. 14. *Publishers Weekly* is published by R.R. Bowker Co., which is owned by Xerox.

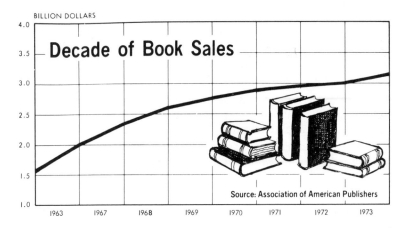

BILLION DOLLARS

Decade of Book Sales

Source: Association of American Publishers

| | 1963 | 1967 | 1968 | 1969 | 1970 | 1971 | 1972 | 1973 |

copies sold. An established author of trade books might be paid 10 per cent of the book's selling price on the first 5,000 sold, 12½ per cent on the next 5,000 and 15 per cent on all beyond 10,000. The author's advance is deducted from his royalty. In the late 1960s, a first novel might bring a $2,000 advance; today it would be closer to $5,000. An established author could expect $7,000 to $10,000 five years ago; he or she is likely to receive $20,000 now. Proven best-selling authors rate much higher advances, often over $1 million.

Many publishers also want to reduce the discounts they give to those who sell their books. These discounts vary by the type and number of books that are ordered. Retailers receive discounts averaging 40 to 43 per cent on trade books; the larger reduction is generally limited to orders of 1,000 or more. Discounts for professional books are generally 20 to 25 per cent. In addition, wholesalers are usually given discounts of about 5 per cent.

Retailers can return unsold books to the publisher after a specified time for a full refund. Many publishing companies, in an effort to save the cost of shipping, storing or destroying these books, are allowing them to be sold to remainder houses which then pass them along to retailers. *Business Week* magazine reported last Sept. 30 that remaindering, once considered unsavory by publishers and authors, "has proved so successful at boosting sales that some books are being reprinted in new editions for remaindering."

Profits come from the relatively few books that become so popular they require reprinting or whose rights are sold to book clubs, paperback publishers, magazines, movies or television. "More and more the source of income for books is not their original hardcover sales in the marketplace but what the book publishing industry calls subsidiary rights," Wayne Warga

111

wrote in the *Los Angeles Times* on March 30, 1975. "Magazines will pay large sums to reprint portions of books, while others pay similarly large amounts to condense portions of the same book. The book clubs can also generate considerable income for a book by selecting it. A book earning $35,000 in royalties (including advance) can earn up to $250,000 in subsidiary rights, rights in which the original publisher and author share."

Lower Cost Options: Book Clubs and Paperbacks

The first book club in America was the Book of the Month Club, founded by Harry Scherman in 1926 and modeled on existing outlets in Germany. The Literary Guild was set up a few years later and others followed, bringing the current number to over 160. By the early 1970s, these clubs were selling almost 100 million books a year to 30 million members. Annual sales were about $250 million. The clubs generally offer a number of books to new members for a nominal fee and require them to choose others for which they pay more, but still less than regular bookstore prices.

The largest of these clubs are the Book of the Month and Readers Digest Condensed Books, with over a million members each, and Literary Guild, a subsidiary of Doubleday, with 800,000. They are able through savings in production and distribution costs to pay substantial sums to the original publishers who split the money 50-50 with the author. Selection by a book club assures publishers of more money for the paperback rights to their books.

Sales of adult paperbacks have more than tripled in the past ten years, climbing faster than any other major category, as is shown in the following figures reported by the Association of American Publishers on book sales, 1964-1974:

Category	Increase	Category	Increase
Adult		Book clubs	83%
paperbacks	261%	Religious	54
Business books	144	Encyclopedias	31
Trade books	102	Juvenile	5

This growth has brought a new respectability to paperbacks, which was evident in a decision by *The New York Times* late last year to review paperbacks each month in its Sunday Book Review section. It is estimated that text and trade paperbacks will account for about 75 per cent of all books published this year, up from 50 per cent eight years ago.

Paperback growth has brought about several changes in softcover publishing. These include the emergence of higher-priced, quality paperbacks alongside the less expensive mass-market offerings; demands by some authors that they, not their

MILLION DOLLARS

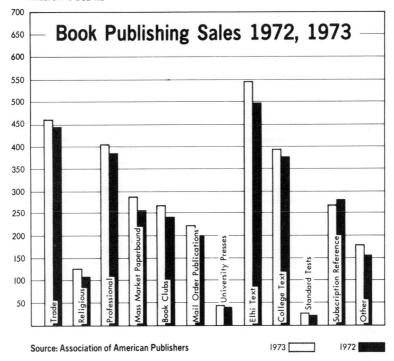

Book Publishing Sales 1972, 1973

Source: Association of American Publishers   1973 ☐   1972 ■

publishers, negotiate paperback contracts or that they receive more than the usual 50-50 split of subsidiary income; growth in the number and size of paperback divisions in hardcover houses; the emergence of so-called "instant paperbacks" like Dell's and Bantam's publications of President Nixon's White House transcripts and, perhaps most important, paperback originals.

There are two major reasons for the popularity of paperback books. One is their accessibility in retail outlets. The other is their lower price. But paperback prices have been climbing and there is some indication that book buyers are resisting them. In its annual report on the 1974 paperback market, *Publishers Weekly* reported on Feb. 3, 1975, that the booming paperback business "finally showed some signs of slowing down in 1974.... No sales increases were reported on the scale of previous years."

As a result, some softcover publishers are seeking to reduce their reprint payments to the hardcover houses. Others may join the growing number of publishers who print original paperbacks. In the last few years, more writers have been selling their manuscripts directly to paperback houses. William Goldman received about $1 million from Dell for three original novels. One of every three books published by Avon is an original. Some paperback houses are following the lead of Ban-

113

tam, the softcover leader, which bought William Peter Blatty's *The Exorcist* several years ago, sold the hardcover rights to Harper & Row and published its own version in paperback after the book had become a best-seller.

The recent acquisition of paperback houses by hardcover publishers—Ballantine by Random House and Popular Library by CBS—makes "far closer cooperation between the hardcover and paperback houses" likely, John P. Dessauer wrote last year in *Publishers Weekly*. "These combinations have joined a number already in existence: Simon & Schuster and Pocket Books, Dial/Delacorte and Dell, Putnam and Berkley. The changing kaleidoscope leads Knopf president Robert Gottlieb to quip: 'The more the paperbook houses do what we do, the more they will encounter our problems; the more we do what they do, the more we shall reap of their profits.' "[5]

Uncertainties in the Educational Market Picture

Educational publishing—text and trade books used in schools, and reference books—was the fastest growing segment in the industry in the 1960s. It was also the most stable; publishers knew approximately how many copies they could sell long before the books appeared in print. But they are now faced not only with the same inflationary-recessionary problems trade publishers are encountering, but with market fragmentation, shrinking or static enrollments, excessive competition for markets and opposition to their books from parents or school boards *(see box, p. 121)*. In addition, the federal government has been cutting back on Great Society programs that have provided substantial sums to schools and libraries.[6]

Textbook sales from kindergarten through the college level now account for about $1 billion a year, up from less than $500 million in 1963. For elementary and high schools, schoolbook expenditures represent only about 1 to 2 per cent of total school spending. And while both the price per book and the number sold have increased substantially in the last 15 years, the average after-tax net profit for textbook publishers fell from 8 per cent in 1960 to 6.9 per cent in 1970 and to 5.9 per cent in 1973. They, unlike their counterparts in trade publishing, have fewer paperback rights and other subsidiary options to cushion their losses or increase their profits.

A recent study compiled by John P. Dessauer Inc. for the National Association of College Bookstores, entitled "1973-1974

---

[5] John P. Dessauer, *Publishers Weekly*, Aug. 5, 1974, p. 25.

[6] Reductions in federal educational funding requested in President Ford's budget for the fiscal year starting July 1, 1975, included (the current level of spending in parentheses : school library resources, $5 million ($92.5 million); library services and construction, $24 million ($49.1 million); and bilingual teaching $15 million ($84.2 million). To be eliminated were $2.5 million for inter-library loans and $9.9 million for college library resources.

Estimated Textbook Sales, 1973

(in thousands of dollars)

State	Sales	Per Student	State	Sales	Per Student
Ala.	$ 7,632	$ 9.22	Mo.	$13,499	$12.05
Alaska	909	10.69	Mont.	2,073	10.91
Ariz.	5,245	10.30	Neb.	4,014	10.88
Ark.	7,150	15.24	Nev.	1,541	11.50
Calif.	29,968	6.27	N.H.	1,963	10.17
Colo.	5,808	9.63	N.J.	20,878	12.04
Conn.	8,099	10.61	N.M.	3,257	11.04
Del.	1,601	10.60	N.Y.	48,671	11.58
D.C.	2,724	17.02	N.C.	16,627	14.13
Fla.	16,353	10.18	N.D.	2,061	13.56
Ga.	11,391	10.25	Ohio	21,182	7.83
Hawaii	1,900	9.45	Okla.	7,837	12.78
Idaho	1,842	9.75	Ore.	13,079	9.91
Ill.	34,638	12.59	Pa.	32,791	11.64
Ind.	16,238	12.38	R.I.	2,080	9.28
Iowa	7,592	10.72	S.C.	8,552	13.22
Kan.	4,966	9.83	S.D.	1,908	11.03
Ky.	8,938	11.64	Tenn.	8,156	8.89
La.	7,135	7.34	Texas	32,143	11.37
Maine	2,747	10.89	Utah	2,860	9.28
Md.	8,189	8.01	Vt.	1,017	8.77
Mass.	14,393	10.41	Va.	13,978	12.49
Mich.	20,673	8.49	Wash.	—	—
Minn.	10,252	10.12	W. Va.	3,508	8.41
Miss.	6,671	11.38	Wis.	11,985	10.27
			Wyo.	909	10.49

SOURCE: Association of American Publishers

Merchandising/Operating Survey," found that price increases had not kept pace with production costs. The average price of a college textbook rose from $4.31 in 1970 to $5.42 in 1974, some 25 per cent. But production costs—paper, printing and binding—increased by 30 per cent during that time. Paper alone, which accounts for 40 per cent of the publishers' manufacturing expense, rose 77 per cent in price.

Before 1960, most educational publishers dealt exclusively with textbooks. Since that time, major trade publishers have set up or expanded their education divisions. Only one of the top five textbook publishers, Scott, Foresman, is devoted exclusively to the educational market. The other four—McGraw-Hill, Houghton Mifflin, Harcourt Brace Jovanovich, and Holt, Rinehart and Winston—also have large trade divisions. Trade publishing's involvement in education has encouraged fragmentation of the traditional textbook market. Schools have been using an increasing number of hardcover and softcover trade books and audiovisual material.

The elementary and high school market is served by several book clubs. The leading one, Scholastic Magazines Inc., distributes more than 50 million trade paperbacks to almost three-fourths of the country's elementary schools and half of the high schools. The growing number of publishers competing on the state and local levels[7] for the education dollar and the sums of money involved in having their books chosen have occasionally led to scandal. Florida's former education commissioner, Floyd T. Christian, pleaded no contest in state court, March 11, 1975, to three charges of accepting $29,000 in kickbacks for a contract involving a $487,000 reading program published by Random House. On April 11, Christian was sentenced to seven years' probation and to pay $43,273 in fines and reparations.

Two publishing categories which are not strictly educational are the university presses and the Government Printing Office (GPO). University presses, most of which are heavily subsidized, primarily publish scholarly books believed to be too unprofitable for trade publication. Due partly to outmoded methods of printing and lack of distribution networks, many of the smaller presses are in dire financial straits; a few have stopped operations entirely and even the larger, wealthier ones have been cutting back on the number of books they publish.

GPO, the world's largest publishing house, could probably qualify as the most inefficient. More than 90 per cent subsidized by the federal government, GPO operations cost $321.3 million in 1973. That year, only about 15 per cent of all publications or about 79 million books and pamphlets were sold. Sixty-five million were distributed free to Congress or government agencies and 14 million to depository libraries.[8]

Changing Image of the Business

PUBLISHING, in its broadest sense, can be traced to the copies of manuscripts made on papyrus or parchment and sold to the public by scribes or slaves in ancient Egypt, Greece and Rome. Publishing, in a modern sense, began in China in the 11th century and in Europe in the 15th century with the invention of

---

[7] In more than a dozen primarily southern and western states, the largest of which are California, Florida and Texas, textbooks are adopted on a statewide basis.

[8] For a critical appraisal of the GPO, see "A Very Odd Publishing House," by Frank Warner in *The Nation,* March 22, 1975, pp. 339-340. Warner is a member of Ralph Nader's Corporate Responsibility Group.

printing from moveable type. Most of the early books off the presses were reprints and compilations; few original works were published.

In the American colonies, the first printing press was set up by Stephen Daye in 1639, two decades after the Pilgrims landed at Plymouth Rock. The first publishing house, established in 1683, for years produced only psalm books, catechisms, sermons and almanacs. England supplied most of the colonists' reading matter, but the native publishing industry grew steadily. By 1755, there were 24 printing presses, publishing 1,200 titles a year, most of them reprints of British books. Itinerant peddlers helped distribute these books.

"Book publishing, they used to say, was the trade of gentlemen. But then sometime in the late 1950s and early 1960s, it acquired glamour rating as an investment. The corporations bought in."

Judith R. Lusic, *The Village Voice,*
Nov. 14, 1974

The difficulties that lexicographer Noah Webster encountered in having his first work published in 1783 give a picture of book publishing at that time. There were no copyright laws and Webster was forced to campaign in various states for laws to protect authors. Having succeeded in Connecticut, he contracted with Hartford printers to issue 5,000 copies of his book, *The Grammatical Institute of the English Language.* The contract obligated Webster to print the books at his own risk and expense. He was, in effect, the author, copyright owner and publisher of his own work. He also "became its chief salesman, and actually peddled the book from town to town."[9]

Imported works continued to account for most of the books sold in the United States until the late 19th century. Sir Walter Scott had so large a following that his American publishers posted agents in England to rush advance sheets of his novels across the ocean. Publishers sold books by Scott, James Fenimore Cooper, Washington Irving and others for $1 to $2. Improvements in printing in the 1830s and 1840s ushered in the era of the penny press and made it possible to turn out large quantities of cheap unbound books for as little as seven cents.

---

[9] American Textbook Publishers Institute, *Textbooks in Education* (1949), p. 33. The Institute is now part of the AAP.

These and the later "dime novels" were immensely popular. Much of the cheap reprint business was made possible by lack of copyright protection. Publishing piracy was rampant and price-cutting the order of the day. But even after an international copyright agreement was concluded in 1891, cheap reprints continued to flourish. While the reading boom continued through most of the century, the late 1800s was a time of crisis for many publishers.

Rise of Publishing Houses; Gentlemen Publishers

The competition to produce cheaper books, and a series of financial upheavels after the panic of 1873, closed many small houses and put a severe strain on the larger ones. At the turn of the century, Harper & Bros. declared bankruptcy and had to be bailed out by financier J.P. Morgan. Publishers were also concerned about competition from other leisure activities. In 1896, *Publishers Weekly* noted "The bicycle craze is demoralizing the equilibrium of books."

By the early 1900s, book publishing was centered in New York, although such established houses as J.B. Lippincott (founded in 1792) remained in Philadelphia and Little, Brown (1837) in Boston. New York could boast of John Wiley (1807), Harper & Bros. (1815), Putnam (1838), Dodd Mead (1839), Charles Scribner (1848), Dutton (1852), Holt (1866), Macmillan (1869), Barnes & Noble (1873), David McKay (1882) and Doubleday (1897). All of these established publishers faced competition from several new houses. McGraw-Hill was set up in 1909, Prentice-Hall in 1913, Harcourt Brace in 1919, Dell in 1921, Simon & Schuster and W.W. Norton in 1924, and Random House and Viking in 1925.

The 1920s were halcyon years for publishers. Editors became increasingly important in deciding what books would be published. During his long career, Maxwell Perkins of Charles Scribner's, perhaps the best-known editor of all, fought to publish young writers who were considered too bold by his more conservative seniors in publishing. The writers under his tutelage included F. Scott Fitzgerald, Ernest Hemingway and Thomas Wolfe. The so-called Literary Decade reached its crest in 1925, a year which "stands as the most notable 12 months in American publishing history."[10]

The financial records of Simon & Schuster from 1924-1926 reveal how publishing houses spent their money. In 1924, the firm paid a $100 advance to superstar Bill Tilden for a book on

---

[10] Allen Churchill, *The Literary Decade* (1971), p. 179. Books published that year included Sinclair Lewis's *Arrowsmith*, Fitzgerald's *The Great Gatsby*, Theodore Dreiser's *An American Tragedy*, Sherwood Anderson's *Dark Laughter*, Willa Cather's *The Professor's House*, Hemingway's *In Our Time*, John Dos Passos's *Manhattan Transfer* and Amy Lowell's *John Keats*.

tennis. Two years later, it spent $10,946 for advances on more than 30 books. The founders, Richard L. Simon and M. Lincoln Schuster, received weekly salaries of about $20. Advertising costs were $736, higher than most other houses; salesmen's salaries and commissions amounted to $3,325; shipping department salaries were $1,863; phone and telegraph bills were $960, rent was $3,089; editorial and travel expenses were $2,290; and administrative outlays were $74. "The profit before taxes wasn't bad—around 24 per cent of sales."[11]

The 1920s were "unusually kind" to publishers, chronicler Alan Churchill noted. "More than 10,000 books aimed at the general public were published in 1929. Ten years before, only half that number had been available in bookshops. High-priced limited editions were fading away, but people were buying regular editions—at about $2.50—as never before. Publishers, intoxicated by prosperity, advertised their products by airplane skywriting."

The publishing giants often reflected the buoyancy and glitter of the decade. A few, notably Alfred A. Knopf, were indeed gentlemen publishers who saw their books as works of art and brought flair and good taste to their houses. Others, like Horace Liveright of Boni & Liveright, were free-spending, party-giving gamblers who preferred to do business in New York's famous speakeasies. While Liveright had great success with many famous authors,[12] his extravagant spending finally ruined him and he went bankrupt in the 1929 crash.

Paperback Market Growth Since Mid-Century

Book publishing and buying underwent enormous growth after World War II, as is reflected in the total number of new and reprinted titles issued each year:

Year	Titles	Year	Titles
1950	11,022	1965	28,595
1955	12,589	1970	36,071
1960	15,012	1974	40,846

After 1950, book sales increased at about twice the population growth rate. The fastest rise was in the sale of paperbacks. While softcover books were sold throughout the 19th century, the "paperback revolution" is said to date from 1939. That year, Pocket Books issued its first series of 10 reprint titles, and distributed them to newsstands, drug stores and other unac-

---

[11] Albert R. Leventhal, "The 20s: Ah, Those Were the Publishing Days," *Publishers Weekly*, Oct. 14, 1974, p. 38. S&S got its start publishing crossword puzzle books.

[12] Including Theodore Dreiser, Sigmund Freud, Anderson, T.S. Eliot, Ezra Pound, Lewis Mumford, William Faulkner, Dorothy Parker, e.e. cummings, Conrad Aiken and Heywood Broun.

customed outlets where they sold for 25 cents apiece. Within eight years, Pocket Books had sold 200 million copies of 475 titles and other publishers had entered the field. By the late 1950s, mass-circulation paperbacks were selling for 35 to 75 cents and Americans were buying almost one million a day.

A second "paperback revolution" began in the early 1950s when the "quality paperback" began to appear. Quality paperbacks, new titles or reprints that sold for up to three times as much as mass-circulation books, were aimed at a more educated or education-seeking buyer. The man behind the quality paperback was Doubleday editor Jason Epstein, who suggested that the company's underused printing press be used to publish inexpensive but quality Anchor paperbacks. The first four Anchor books, published in 1953 and priced at 85 cents to $1.25, sold 10,-000 copies each in two weeks. Publishing houses that had shown no interest in paperbacks, except for sale of the reprint rights to others, began issuing their own lines. In 1954, Alfred A. Knopf started Vintage and Epstein moved from Anchor to direct it.

A third revolution in paperback publishing came in 1964 when Bantam produced in a remarkably short time the "Report of the Warren Commission," a reprint of the official findings into President Kennedy's death. Aided by improvements in high-speed printing presses, Bantam has published over 50 "instant books" since that time. Last year, both Dell and Bantam came out with versions of the White House Watergate transcripts a week after President Nixon released them. Dell's 736-page paperback sold for $2.45 and Bantam's for $2.50. The Government Printing Office edition was priced at $12.25.

The amount of money paid by paperback houses, particularly the "Big Five"—Bantam, Dell, Fawcett, New American Library and Pocket Books—to publish hardcover titles is indicative of the importance and respectability that paperbacks now have. In 1972, Fawcett paid James Michener $1 million for his novel *The Drifters*. Last year, Warner paid as much to *Washington Post* reporters Carl Bernstein and Bob Woodward for *All the President's Men*. In the late 1940s, Norman Mailer received only $35,000 for the best-seller *The Naked and the Dead*.

Corporate Takeover of Book Publishing Industry

The ever-increasing amount of money needed to run publishing houses resulted in a rash of mergers and takeovers in the late 1950s and 1960s. A student of the business, Herbert S. Bailey, noted that "many publishing houses have merged with or been bought by large electronics companies that can supply capital and that have an interest in what they call the 'knowledge industry.' The companies see the publishing houses not only as sources of profit but also as sources of educational

West Virginia Textbook Hassle

"Down with textbooks—up with God," irate demonstrators in Kanawha County, W.Va., chanted last fall. They were protesting $500,000 worth of new public school books which they labeled "filth, trash, obscene, anti-Christian, anti-American and communistic." The protest kept thousands of children out of school. Several bombings and shootings occurred and some schools and industries were shut down temporarily.

The books in dispute included the series "Communicating" for grades 1-6 and "Dynamics of Learning" for grades 7-12, both published by D.C. Heath; Scott, Foresman's "Galaxy" for grades 7-12; Houghton Mifflin's "Interaction" for grades 7-12 and McDougal-Littell's "Man" for grades 7-12.

Mr. and Mrs. Gary Williams brought a suit challenging the authority of the Kanawha Board of Education to introduce books which, they claimed, violated their First Amendment rights. But U.S. District Court Judge Kenneth K. Hall ruled, Jan. 30, 1975, that while the texts might be offensive to the plaintiffs' beliefs, they did not violate the church-state separation principle.

---

and other materials to fill their educational channels."[13] Electronics company-publishing mergers include RCA and Random House; Holt, Rinehart and Winston and CBS; Wesleyan University Press and Xerox; and Science Research Associates and IBM.

The merger trend was greeted with alarm by publishing purists who feared the corporate giants would publish only those books likely to make a profit. But Alfred A. Knopf, speaking a few years after the merger between Knopf and Random House in 1960, insisted that it "has not affected in the slightest degree our editorial policy. We have continued, without any interference whatever, to publish what we had wanted to publish."[14]

In addition to Knopf, Random House bought Vintage, Pantheon, Ballantine and the textbook house L.W. Singer. Macmillan, the country's fourth largest book publisher, is probably the most diversified publishing conglomerate. Severed from its British parent company in 1952, it subsequently acquired the Berlitz School of Languages, Katherine Gibbs secretarial school, LaSalle Extension University, Brentano's book stores, printing and music companies, art and gift stores, the British publishing house of Cassell & Co., and about 100

[13] Herbert S. Bailey, *The Art and Science of Book Publishing* (1970), pp. 69-70.
[14] Alfred A. Knopf, *Publishing Then and Now: 1912-1964* (1964), p. 23. Under the Knopf-Random House merger, the business departments were combined but editorial departments remained "completely different" and Knopf continued to publish books under its own name.

other companies. Early this year, it set up a performing arts subsidiary to sell to theaters, movies and television, and to record companies.

While the corporate owners may not have lowered the quality of the books being published, they did encourage the publication of many more books. According to John P. Dessauer, the new owners knew little about the industry's problems and "simply imposed their forecasting, budget and accounting methods upon their new subsidiaries and set some very unrealistic revenue and profit goals for them.... There was obviously no hope of ever achieving the projections...so the logical solution appeared to be to publish as many new titles as possible—and pray that a good number of them would turn into best sellers."[15]

Economic Outlook for Publishers

TOO MANY BOOKS? was the title of a three-part series by Dessauer in *Publishers Weekly* last fall. Citing industry figures that the number of books in print had increased from 163,000 in 1963 to 398,000 a decade later—144 per cent—Dessauer suggested that overproducing publishers "decline manuscripts that are poorly written, badly researched, imitative and derivative" and "eliminate mediocre, second-rate books from their lists." Similar proposals were heard as far back as 1880 when only 2,076 books were published.

In the early 1930s, O.H. Cheney authored "An Economic Survey of the Book Industry, 1930-1931," usually referred to as the Cheney Report. He concluded that far too many books were being published and that publishers must make sizable reductions in their lists. Alfred A. Knopf said the same thing in 1964.

Dessauer looked ahead to a time when "new title production has been cut in half."[16] This would mean that bookstores could keep salable books "on display for as long as they show signs of life. Review media are able to do justice to most deserving contenders. Libraries, able to cope with current production, once again are content. Classics and backlist titles are restored to their rightful place.... Publishers' earnings have risen significantly and return on investment has improved substantially.... Authors are happy because their income has risen and their creations are receiving more reader attention."

---

[15] "Too Many Books?" *Publishers Weekly*, Sept. 30, 1974.
[16] *Publishers Weekly*, Oct. 7, 1974.

Dessauer's series provoked a storm of controversy. Authors and academicians argued that a 50 per cent reduction in title output would discourage publishers from accepting quality manuscrips that are unlikely to be profitable. Peter S. Prescott of *Newsweek* magazine wrote in *Publishers Weekly* on Dec. 2: "An indisputable truth remains: when retrenchment comes, the good books are the first to go." Publishers were more irate. In the same issue, W.W. Norton president George P. Brockway contended that "Mr. Dessauer's recommendations are so absurd that there's no danger of their being acted on by the industry as a whole."

But there has been some retrenchment in title output in the past year and this trend is considered almost certain to continue. Other likely developments are improvements in printing technology to make it possible to print fewer copies of a book at lower cost. Low-cost "short runs," the printing of only a few thousand copies, would help eliminate one of the major uncertainties in book publishing, the question of whether a certain book might sell anywhere near the 10,000 or more copies that normally are printed on the initial press run.

Opportunities for Expansion in Education Field

Publishers of educational material are bothered less by title overproduction than by market fragmentation. The basic textbook of a generation ago has been replaced to a large extent by a variety of material including trade paperbacks, compilations of previously published works, audio-visual aids, and so-called continuing education books. Technological improvements in photocopying, microfilm and microfishe[17] are also contributing to the fragmentation.

Some persons in publishing regard the adult-education market as potentially more lucrative than the classroom market.[18] Another possibility for expansion is "demand publishing." Several years ago, Marc Strausberg, a salesman for the college textbook firm of Allyn & Bacon, came up with the idea of letting teachers order custom-made books for their courses. The publisher assembles the material the teacher chooses and has it put in book form in about a month. While demand publishers have encountered some difficulty over reprint rights and copyright laws, Strausberg's Mss Information Corporation published 375 titles in 1973. IBM and Xerox-Simon & Schuster have also been successful in marketing these tailor-made books.

Publishers have been producing slides, films and other non-book products for years, but the audio-visual age did not arrive

---

[17] Microfishe is a piece of film containing information which becomes readable when the film is placed in a reading device. Unlike microfilm, microfishe is not on a reel.
[18] See Paul D. Doebler, "The Brave New World of Adult Education," *Publishers Weekly*, Dec. 30, 1974.

until the mid-1960s when Congress appropriated large sums of money for schools and libraries. Dinoo J. Vanier notes that some of the mergers in the late 1960s—Random House-RCA (1966), Raytheon-D.C. Heath (1966), CBS-Holt, Rinehart and Winston (1966), Bell and Howell-Charles E. Merrill (1967), and Xerox-R.R. Bowker (1968)—"were brought about by a strong belief by the principals that a combination of audio-visual and printed materials leading to integrated educational systems would more appropriately serve future markets."[19] Virtually all major book publishers now market audio-visual equipment.

A number of them, alarmed at "uncontrolled duplication" which makes it possible to produce their books and audio-visual material quickly and inexpensively, have formed a Coalition for Fair Copyright Protection. In a statement issued March 24, 1975, this group of publishers urged the enactment of "a strong, modern copyright law to cope with a new technological age." Complaining about "piracy on a national scale," the publishers held that "the copier becomes a publisher who assumes all the advantages and none of the responsibilities." The coalition will lobby for copyright revision bills pending in Congress.

Some persons in the industry also see microfilm and microfishe as a threat to book publishing, particularly in the library and school markets. Others, however, believe that publishers should be involved in producing microfilm and microfishe as a hedge against rising paper prices or shortages and storage costs. *Industry Week* magazine noted last Sept. 30 that 2,000 pages of a standard textbook fits on a four-by-six-inch microfishe card and could be read anywhere in a machine that costs about $25.

Possible Sales Growth in Foreign Book Markets

With book sales lagging in this country, publishers are eagerly looking to foreign markets. In 1973, the last year for which figures are available, the Department of Commerce estimated that book-export sales, excluding shipments valued under $250 and income from rights and translations, amounted to $194.5 million, 13 per cent more than the year before. The industry speculates that if shipments under $250 were included, sales would have been $292.5 million, more than 9 per cent of total publishing receipts.[20]

While export sales have risen sharply in recent years, there are several reasons why this growth may not continue. One is the relatively high price of American books. Another is the amount of publishing activity in other countries, including the

---

[19] Dinoo J. Vanier, *Market Structure and the Business of Book Publishing* (1973), p. 30.
[20] In the same year, book imports of over $250 declined by 2.2 per cent to $133.8 million; all book imports, it is estimated, came to about $147 million.

development nations of Asia, Africa and Latin America. In India, for example, the literacy rate has increased from 13 per cent in 1947 to almost 50 per cent today. Largely as a result, there are now at least 11,000 firms publishing more than 14,000 titles a year in India. Increasing literacy and nationalism have spurred publication of books in the national language, Hindi, and encouraged some resistance to imported works.[21]

Nationalistic currents are also affecting America's largest foreign market, Canada. Campbell Hughes, president of Van Nostrand Reinhold of Canada, told an AAP seminar in New York on March 10 that Canada buys almost half of the books the United States exports. But Canadians resent "foreign domination of the publishing industry," he said, and "the percentage of imported as opposed to locally produced books will move inexorably downward."

Major U.S. publishers are concerned about an antitrust suit filed by the Justice Department last Nov. 25 charging them with conspiring with British publishers to divide up world markets for English-language books. The 21 U.S. defendants include Bantam, Dell, Doubleday, Harcourt Brace Jovanovich, Harper & Row, Macmillan, McGraw-Hill, Random House, and Simon & Schuster. The British Publishers Association and a number of British publishers were named as co-conspirators.

Viability of Small, Special-Interest Publishers

As book publishing becomes more fragmented, some observers see signs of a new era which will witness the decline of the large, New York-based conglomerates and the emergence of small, special-interest firms. There are now over 150 of these small houses on the West Coast, specializing in a variety of subjects from radical feminism to Buddhism, from gardening to railroads. Another recent development is the establishment of non-profit groups like the New York-based Fiction Collective. Modeled on Sweden's author cooperatives, Fiction Collective was set up in 1973 by a group of young authors who edit, design, copyread, publish, advertise and distribute their own fiction.

Some believe that the trend in book publishing in the next decade will be not mergers but less-formal liaisons between the large conglomerates and smaller publishing houses. The relationship between Random House and Bookworks, an unconventional San Francisco firm specializing in titles on physical and spiritual well-being, is one of a growing number of such arrangements. Random House determines the size of the printing, the price of the book and the jacket design and undertakes printing, marketing and distribution.

---

[21] See "World Literary Survey," *Saturday Review,* April 19, 1975.

The next few years are likely to witness numerous changes and innovations in the book publishing business. Economic conditions will force publishers to find less expensive ways of printing their books and running their houses. Fewer marginally profitable works will be accepted and fewer established writers will be able to command million-dollar advances. Book publishers, like other businessmen, know only too well that the free-spending sprees that characterized the late 1960s cannot be sustained in this time of retrenchment.

Selected Bibliography

Books

The American Textbook Publishers Institute, *Textbooks in Education*, The American Textbook Publishers Institute, 1949.

Bailey, Herbert S. Jr., *The Art and Science of Book Publishing*, Harper & Row, 1970.

Bingley, Clive, *The Business of Book Publishing*, Pergamon Press, 1972.

Churchill, Allen, *The Literary Decade*, Prentice-Hall, 1971.

Grannis, Chandler B. (ed.), *What Happens in Book Publishing*, Columbia University Press, 1957.

Knopf, Alfred A., *Publishing Then and Now: 1912-1964*, The New York Public Library, 1964.

Tebbel, John, *A History of Book Publishing in the United States*, Vol. II, Bowker, 1975.

Vanier, Dinoo J., *Market Structure and the Business of Book Publishing*, Pitman, 1973.

Articles

Anreder, Steven S., "Harcourt Brace Slated to Extend Earnings Gains," *Barron's*, March 3, 1975.

Elias, Christopher, "Are Things Better at McGraw-Hill?" *Commercial & Financial Chronicle*, May 6, 1974.

"Fallen Leaves," *The Guardian*, March 1, 1975.

Fremont-Smith, Eliot, "How's Business? Not Bad. How's Fiction? Don't Ask," *New York*, Feb. 3, 1975.

Lusic, Judith R., "Strange Times in the Book Trade," *The Village Voice*, Nov. 14, 1974.

Pace, Eric, "Publishers Can't Balance the Books," *Moneysworth*, Feb. 3, 1975.

"Printing-Publishing Firms Expect Continued Growth," *Commerce Today*, Feb. 3, 1975.

Publishers Weekly, selected issues.

Smith, Lee, "Business and the Vanity Press," *Dun's*, June 1974.

Warner, Frank, "A Very Odd Publishing House," *The Nation*, March 22, 1975.

Williamson, Chilton, Jr., "The Weals and Woes of University Presses," *Commonweal*, May 24, 1974.

Reports and Studies

The Bowker Annual of Library & Book Trade Information, 1974.

Cheney, O. H., "Economic Survey of the Book Industry, 1930-1931."

Literary Market Place, 74-75, 1974.

PART 3
Government Action

FEDERAL FISCAL CONTROL

by

David Boorstin

1 9 7 5
Jan. 17

FEDERAL FISCAL CONTROL

T HE MOST SERIOUS threat to the American and the
world economy in a generation faces President Ford as he
draws up the fiscal 1976 federal budget for presentation to the
new 94th Congress.[1] Federal budget making is often described
as the process of setting national priorities. In its broadest
interpretation, the budget represents the administration's view
of what role the government should play in the nation's economic and social system and in world affairs. In a narrower
sense, government fiscal policies represent a choice of strate-
gies for achieving these objectives: should defense allocations
go to nuclear or conventional forces? Should the poor be aided
by food stamps, cash assistance or tax benefits?

These important questions are currently overshadowed by the
problem of how to use fiscal policy to ease the nation's economic
plight. While most prices rose less rapidly than in earlier
months, a sign that inflation might be weakening, unemployment jumped from 6 per cent in October to 7.1 per cent in
December, the highest rate in 13 years, representing 6.5 million
unemployed Americans—the highest total since 1940. Many
observers predicted a rise to 8 per cent in 1975, amounting to the
most massive layoffs since the Depression Thirties.

As the job picture deteriorated, pressures increased on President Ford to switch from a tight fiscal policy aimed at controlling inflation to a stimulative one aimed at offsetting recession.
Toward the year end, there were clear signs that the administration was changing its economic policy.[2] Exactly what path
should be taken and how far the government should go remained a subject of debate among politicians and economists.

Then in a nationally televised address on Jan. 13, President
Ford proposed anti-recession tax cuts totaling $16 billion, com-

---

[1] The President is required by law to send an annual budget to Congress within 15 days of
the opening of each regular session, unless an extension is granted. The 1974 session opened
Jan. 14.
[2] Presidential Press Secretary Ron Nessen confirmed to newsmen on Jan. 8 a change was
forthcoming from inflation-fighting to pump-priming. He was reminded that Ford had told
the Business Council in New York on Dec. 11 that there would be no "180 degree turn" with
recession replacing inflation as "public enemy no. 1." "Well, it could be 179 degrees," Nessen
answered.

posed of $12 billion in rebates on 1974 tax payments by individuals and $4 billion in tax relief for corporations. In addition Ford called for higher taxes on natural gas and oil to encourage energy conservation and provide $30 billion annually in federal revenues. These would be returned to the economy in the form of additional tax cuts and payments, including aid to the poor. To demonstrate fiscal restraint, Ford said he would veto any new spending programs in 1975, and insisted on a 5 per cent limit for increases in Social Security benefits, government and military pay.

The President's message came just a few hours after congressional Democratic leaders had made public their own "emergency" economic program, including a "substantial" tax cut and faster spending for public works. Rep. Al Ullman (D Ore.), new chairman of the House Ways and Means Committee, had previously predicted that his committee would produce a tax-cut bill by March 1. Passage could be delayed for weeks or months, however, by disagreements about what form a tax reduction should take, and in particular by Senate Finance Committee opposition to ending the oil depletion allowance.[3]

A quick tax cut is viewed as a way to prevent the recession from getting out of hand before the forces of recovery take hold, lifting incomes and consumer confidence which is now at its lowest postwar level. It would offset the "fiscal drag" caused by inflation which not only erodes purchasing power but pushes taxpayers with nominally higher incomes into higher tax brackets. Charles L. Schultze of the Brookings Institution, budget director in the Johnson administration, observed that in the 18 months from early 1973 to late 1974 inflation raised taxes by $34 billion a year, putting the brakes on the economy just as it was tipping into a recession and needed stimulus.[4]

Although some Ford advisers fear that excessive tax relief might rekindle inflation, Chairman Alan Greenspan of the Council of Economic Advisers has said "rapid and timely action to reduce taxes" is needed.[5] Schultze, at Brookings, said that a tax cut of over $20 billion would be necessary to offset the current slump, while many others put the figure as high as $30 billion. The tax cut pushed by President Johnson in 1964 is often taken as an example of how tax cuts can successfully increase consumer spending and stimulate investment. It has been pointed out that it would take a $27 billion tax reduction now to equal—as a percentage of gross national product—the $11.5 billion annual cut enacted in 1964.

[3] See "Oil Taxation," *E.R.R.*, 1974 Vol. I, pp. 203-220.
[4] Quoted in *The Washington Post*, Jan. 4, 1974.
[5] Quoted in *U.S. News & World Report*, Dec. 30, 1974, p. 8.

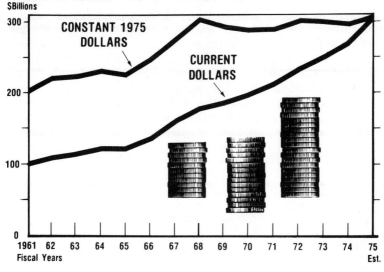

FEDERAL BUDGET OUTLAYS 1961-75

$Billions

CONSTANT 1975 DOLLARS

CURRENT DOLLARS

300

200

100

0

1961 62 63 64 65 66 67 68 69 70 71 72 73 74 75
Fiscal Years   Est.

It is argued that by stimulating consumption, production and employment—and hence federal tax revenues—a tax cut need not add to the 1976 federal deficit by its full amount. If a tax cut had its intended effect, it could even shrink the deficit in fiscal 1977 just as the 1964 tax cut helped shrink the deficit in fiscal 1965 below prior estimates. Some persons contend, however, that taxpayers may not significantly alter their spending habits if they know the tax changes are temporary. Furthermore, any losses in revenue would have to be at least partially offset, for example by raising gasoline taxes or by ending certain tax preferences, in order to allay concern in Congress and the White House over huge federal budget deficits.

The Joint Economic Committee of Congress, in a staff study released Dec. 31, 1974, forecast a $23 billion deficit for the current fiscal year even without a tax cut.[6] Yet no one knows just how severely the business slump will affect tax receipts. One uncertain factor is a switch in accounting procedures by many corporations to last-in, first-out accounting (LIFO). This change reduces the taxable "inventory profits" resulting from the escalating value of stocks on hand in an inflationary period. Government analysts said the new accounting could trim tax revenues as much as $4 billion in 1975. Sen. William Proxmire (D Wis.), a committee member, said that if half of all corporations make the change, the loss will be $6 billion to $9 billion.[7]

[6] In his State of the Union address on Jan. 15, Ford put the fiscal 1975 deficit figure at about $30 billion, and the fiscal 1976 deficit at $45 billion, including the tax cuts.

[7] *The Wall Street Journal*, Nov. 11 and Nov. 21, 1974.

As economic conditions worsen, not only the likelihood but the desirability of balancing the budget is questioned. It is recalled that President Kennedy, influenced by the "new economics" of adviser Walter Heller and others, broke with tradition in 1963 and proposed a deliberately unbalanced budget for fiscal 1964 to stimulate a lagging economy; the economy perked up sufficiently to reduce Kennedy's projected $11.9 billion deficit to $5.9 billion. In the Ford administration, Roy L. Ash told the Senate Budget Committee on Dec. 12, as director of the Office of Management and Budget,[8] that the administration would not insist on spending cuts to balance the 1976 budget in the face of lagging revenues. The Joint Economic Committee report forecast a $36 billion deficit in fiscal 1976 even without a tax cut, simply to maintain the 1975 level of services. This would be the biggest peacetime deficit in the nation's history.[9]

The report said, however, that the projected deficit for fiscal 1976 "represents a rather neutral fiscal policy." The projected $36 billion deficit "will not stimulate the economy back toward our potential standard." The deficit increase represented revenues lost and expenditures increased as a result of higher unemployment, rather than as a result of positive fiscal policy. If the economy were at its "full employment" level—the level when unemployment is no higher than 4 per cent—the 1976 budget would show a $30 billion surplus, representing no change from a projected full-employment surplus for fiscal 1975.

Limits on Budget Decisions; Unemployment Factor

Large as the current federal budget is—Ford projected $314 billion for fiscal 1975—government spending is not much larger than in 1968 in terms of constant dollars adjusted for inflation.[10] Since then, however, the character of the budget has changed, with a growing predominance of "mandatory" over "discretionary" expenditures. As was noted in the 1975 budget:

> In 1967, 59 per cent of total federal spending was virtually uncontrollable due to existing laws or prior legal commitments. Since then, repeated increases in uncontrollable programs have been enacted into law.... In 1975, about 74 per cent of the budget will be virtually uncontrollable. Of this amount, 78 per cent are "open-ended programs and fixed costs," which includes social security, general revenue sharing, interest on the federal debt, veterans benefits, and similar programs.[11]

---

[8] On Jan. 1, Ford nominated James T. Lynn, Secretary of Housing and Urban Development, to replace Ash, who had resigned but remained in office to complete the 1976 budget.

[9] The record budget deficit was $53.8 billion in 1943, during World War II. The record postwar budget deficit was $25.1 billion in 1968.

[10] However, on a constant-dollar basis, federal expenditures increased about 50 per cent from 1961 to 1968.

[11] *The Budget of the United States Government, Fiscal Year 1975*, pp. 38-39.

COMPOSITION OF REAL FEDERAL OUTLAYS
(CONSTANT 1975 DOLLARS)

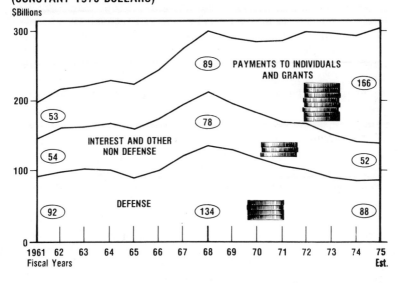

$Billions

PAYMENTS TO INDIVIDUALS AND GRANTS — 89, 166

INTEREST AND OTHER NON DEFENSE — 53, 78, 54, 52

DEFENSE — 92, 134, 88

1961 62 63 64 65 66 67 68 69 70 71 72 73 74 75

Fiscal Years   Est.

Thus, with about three-quarters of federal spending beyond executive control, budget makers increasingly find their choices pre-empted. Ash sees this as the major budgetary issue. According to his figures, if the average 9 per cent growth rate in these mandatory and "transfer payments"[12] continues unchanged through the year 2000, federal and state and local budgets will amount to two-thirds of the gross national product. "What kind of a society will we have if two-thirds of the economy comes through the government?" he asked.[13] Less conservative experts, too, are beginning to worry about increases in Social Security, unemployment, and other benefits, especially as these are partially or fully financed by payroll taxes which are generally seen as regressive.[14] Ash has raised the question whether such payments to individuals should be reduced.

Such reductions are unlikely in the face of a recessionary situation, when unemployment compensation and other welfare transfers serve to stabilize the economy. In addition to tax cuts, welfare and public works expenditures are the two principal weapons of discretionary fiscal policy. Congress in its 1974 post-election session used these two weapons in an attempt to alleviate the impact of recession. Congress set up an emergency public jobs program and extended unemployment compensation

---

[12] "Transfer payments" are funds disbursed by the government for which no services are rendered; they represent not purchases but rather the transfer of money from taxpayers to certain needy or worthy groups to further social ends.
[13] Quoted in *The Washington Post*, Nov. 24, 1974.
[14] See "Social Security Financing," *E.R.R.*, 1972 Vol. II, pp. 707-724.

coverage to approximately 12 million persons currently ineligible; gave unemployed workers an additional 13 weeks of benefits; and appropriated $4 billion in fiscal 1975 to fund the programs.[15] The Joint Economic Committee estimated that payments to the unemployed, including the new legislation, would be $5.3 billion higher in fiscal 1975 than was estimated when the budget was presented to Congress in February 1974. Assuming an average unemployment rate of 7.2 per cent for calendar year 1975, an additional growth of $5.2 billion in fiscal 1976 was predicted.

While proposals for public job programs receive widespread support, some analysts are skeptical of the ability of these programs to boost the economy substantially. "By providing an average salary of $7,500 to $8,500 a year, a $4 billion annual program would create about 500,000 jobs, representing less than 1 per cent...unemployment," economic writer Robert J. Samuelson calculated. He contended that the program "is intended to be a temporary Novocain for the recession, designed as much to avoid the appearance of being callous as to bring down unemployment."[16] There are fears that after six months or a year more than 50 per cent of the "new" jobs may be lost through the "displacement effect"—city and state officials using federal funds to hire people they would have hired anyway.

The Ford administration, opposing programs that might become permanent sources of federal money for state and local jobs, implicitly favors "make-work" jobs which can be easily phased out later. Many cities, however, have already been forced by financial problems to lay off existing employees: New York, for example, facing at least a $430 million deficit in its $12.8 billion budget, has eliminated 7,900 jobs, or about 3 per cent of the city's work force. Thus there is confusion over how much of the federal job money could go to rehire workers the cities have recently fired.

While many policymakers feel that a public jobs program will provide some relief for unemployment, there are doubts as to its effectiveness on the present scale unless it is combined with other stimulative policies. At the same time some economists, such as Milton Friedman of the "Chicago School,"[17] fear that the government's need to finance job programs will lead to further inflationary pressures which in the long run will produce even more unemployment. The fundamental question is whether a prolonged period of high unemployment is actually necessary to

---

[15] See *Congressional Quarterly Weekly Report*, Dec. 21, 1974, pp. 3363-3369.

[16] Writing in *The Washington Post*, Dec. 15, 1974.

[17] Named for Friedman, economics professor at the University of Chicago, and other monetary theorists he has influenced. They view the rate of growth of the money supply as the key determinant of the direction and quality of economic change.

bring down inflation; and if so, at how high a level and for how long.

Impact of Inflation on U.S. Defense Expenditures

Probably the most important of the allocative decisions embodied in the budget is the division of outlays between national security and domestic objectives. Budgeting for defense is also one of the most controversial matters: the issues are complex, information is frequently inadequate, and decisions must be made not only on the basis of American need but on how they will be interpreted by allies and rivals. "In sum, judgments about the relationship between alternative military postures and the achievement of foreign policy objectives, much more than technical military considerations, are the major determinants of the size of the investment in national security."[18]

The economic pressures caused by inflation are now leading to a reevaluation of defense policy in terms of how much defense the nation needs and can afford. Like everything else, defense costs have been going up: the Defense Department calculates it will need an additional $10 billion in fiscal 1976 just to offset inflation. Although defense spending has been growing about 6 per cent annually in the last few years, the Pentagon argues that in terms of constant dollars, defense spending is currently 40 per cent below the 1968 level and 18 per cent below the pre-Vietnam level of 1964; since 1964 it has declined from 42 per cent of the federal budget to 27 per cent, and from 8.3 per cent of gross national product to 6 per cent.

The Soviet military program is reported to be growing in real terms at a rate of 3 to 5 per cent a year, and Pentagon planners fear that without a substantial increase in the U.S. defense budget the military balance of power might be lost—not by policy but by the erosion of purchasing power.

The defense budget, like other aspects of the federal budget, is stated in two different ways: a statement of planned "outlays" (actual spending) during a fiscal year, and a request for "new obligational authority" (authority to commit the government to spend money) in the current and future fiscal years. Defense outlays are currently running at about $84 billion, and the Ford administration was reportedly planning to ask Congress for a record $95 billion for outlays in fiscal 1976. Requests for new obligational authority, however, would be about $103 billion. Thus the President would find himself in the difficult position of proposing the first three-digit defense budget to a Democratic

---

[18] Barry H. Blechman, Edward M. Gramlich, and Robert W. Hartman, *Setting National Priorities: The 1975 Budget* (Brookings Institution, 1974), p. 132. See also "Peacetime Defense Spending" *E.R.R.*, 1974 Vol. I, pp. 263-282.

Congress at a time of mounting deficits, and with critics contending that there is considerable waste in defense spending.

But the critics do not agree where cuts could or should be made. While some maintain that billions are being wasted in the purchase of unneeded or poorly designed weapons, others look hard at personnel expenditures. Manpower costs now account for 56 per cent of the defense budget, up from 43 per cent ten years ago. The military forces are 15 per cent below the 1964 pre-Vietnam level but the payroll is more than double. Even if areas of waste can be identified and cut out, there is still the question of whether this should lead to reductions in the defense budget or to the reallocation of those funds to defense programs which would provide added combat capability and flexibility.[19]

Operation of Federal Budget System

THE FEDERAL BUDGET is a relatively new institution of government. The first Secretary of the Treasury, Alexander Hamilton, tried briefly to coordinate executive branch money proposals, but his plan was soon abandoned. Through the succeeding years the various agencies of government dealt directly with congressional committees on their individual budgets. During most of the 19th century, with the exception of the Civil War period, federal revenues came mainly from customs duties and grew faster than expenditures.

These conditions prevailed until toward the end of the century, when the Spanish-American War and new demands for federal services began to produce deficits. The government went into debt in 10 of the 16 fiscal years between 1894 and 1909. Muckrakers of the period, agitating for reforms, prompted President Taft to appoint in 1910 a Commission on Economy and Efficiency. The commission's report, two years later, urged that a federal budget system be set up.

The recommended action was finally taken under the terms of the Budget and Accounting Act of 1921. That legislation (1) directed the President to prepare and submit to Congress an annual budget giving complete information on the condition of revenues and expenditures, (2) created the Bureau of the Budget to act as agent of the President in preparing the budget, and (3) created the General Accounting Office as an arm of Congress to review government spending. "This piece of legislation has been

---

[19] See Philip Odeen, "In Defense of the Defense Budget," *Foreign Policy*, fall 1974, pp. 93-108.

considered the most important fiscal reform enacted in the United States in the 20th century," the Tax Foundation has observed. "Prior to this time the United States, alone among the important nations of the world, had not developed a system of overall national government budgeting."[20]

The first budget director, Charles G. Dawes, in the words of his successors, "marked out a limited area of responsibility, and for more than a decade after he left office [in 1922] the bureau held pretty much to the Dawes pattern....The bureau as we know it today was formed in the latter half of the Thirties."[21] Franklin D. Roosevelt began using the Budget Bureau "in coordinating the activities of the governmental agencies, rather than relying upon it strictly for...holding down government expenditures—which had been almost its sole function under his predecessors."[22]

At Roosevelt's insistence, Congress passed the Administrative Reorganization Act of 1939, which moved the bureau from the Treasury to the newly established Executive Office of the President. Until that time, the bureau had had an average of only 38 to 42 staff members. Expansion, required to perform the new duties placed on the bureau by Roosevelt and by the coming of World War II, soon began. But even today the agency is small by Washington standards, with about 660 employees and a budget of $21 million in fiscal 1975. Its power has nevertheless continued to grow.

Bureau's Reorganization Under President Nixon

In 1970, Congress approved a reorganization plan submitted by President Nixon to establish an Office of Management and Budget (OMB) to be built around the nucleus of the budget bureau, which was abolished. Nixon's decision to establish OMB was the first rearrangement of a President's traditional relationship with his cabinet officers and his budget officials in 31 years. It extended the budgeting functions, aiming to make greater use of organization and management systems. The purpose was to provide greater executive capability for analyzing, coordinating, evaluating and improving the efficiency of expanding government programs.

The office's new functions were to include assisting with the implementation of major legislation (such as environmental programs) under which several agencies share responsibility; coordinating the complex system of federal grants which often

[20] Tax Foundation, *Controlling Federal Expenditures*, December 1963, p. 9.
[21] Budget Director David E. Bell in a speech June 9, 1961, the 40th anniversary of President Harding's approval of the Budget and Accounting Act.
[22] A.J. Wann, "Franklin D. Roosevelt and the Bureau of the Budget," *Business and Government Review*, March-April 1968, p. 33.

involve a variety of federal, state and local agencies; and evaluating the cost-effectiveness of particular programs and the relative priority of needs they were designed to meet. Some observers thought that another rationale for OMB was to strengthen the budget planners' ability to question defense spending requests. Despite sizable cuts by OMB in the fiscal 1972 defense budget, however, this purpose was never formally confirmed by the Nixon administration.[23]

Because of his preoccupation with the Watergate scandal during the last two years of his administration, President Nixon largely disengaged himself from the budgeting process. This led to criticism that the OMB itself had become an advocate of policy rather than a politically neutral analytical tool. It was called a monolithic superagency imposing budgetary decisions based on political considerations on other federal agencies and departments. For this reason the team appointed by President Ford to smooth his transition into the White House recommended that the powers of the OMB be substantially curtailed. This recommendation was later withdrawn, however. It was said that Ford's active interest in the budgetary process was returning the bureau to its more traditional role.

Process of Budget Making in Executive Branch

The visible part of the OMB's work is the annual budget which the President is required to submit to Congress. But that is only the tip of the iceberg. For a typical fiscal year, the process begins with a "spring preview" in May of the preceding year, when the major agencies and departments submit general projections and look at programs which will demand special attention. Through May and June these are reviewed by OMB examiners assigned to the various agencies, who help them to come up with a total figure.

During this time, other OMB specialists are consulting the Treasury Department and the Council of Economic Advisers about the long-range effects of agency programs on fiscal guidelines set forth in the latest federal budget. After all this information has been accumulated and digested, the budget director begins discussions with the President on the shape of the future budget. These talks tend to become increasingly more frequent as the end of the year approaches and hard decisions can no longer be postponed.

In letters sent to the agencies in August, the OMB sets out budgetary targets and guidelines in accordance with fiscal policy. While smaller agencies or departments may receive only

---

[23] For background about the reorganization and congressional objections, see *Congress and the Nation*, Vol. III (Congressional Quarterly Inc., 1973), pp. 66-69.

Federal Budgets* Since 1960

(in billions of dollars)

Fiscal Year	Outlays	Receipts	Surplus or deficit (−)
1960	92.22	92.49	0.27
1961	97.79	94.38	− 3.40
1962	106.81	99.67	− 7.13
1963	111.31	106.56	− 4.75
1964	118.58	112.66	− 5.92
1965	118.43	116.83	− 1.59
1966	134.65	130.85	− 3.79
1967	158.25	149.55	− 8.70
1968	178.83	153.67	−25.16
1969	184.54	187.78	3.23
1970	196.58	193.74	− 2.84
1971	211.42	188.39	−23.03
1972	231.87	208.64	−23.22
1973	246.52	232.22	−14.30
1974	268.34	264.84	− 3.49

* Figures are stated in terms of the unified budget concept.
Figures in third column may not agree with other two because of rounding.

---

general guidelines, the major ones may be informed of specific policy decisions—for example, the Interior Department might be told that the President intends to increase coal production—and may even be given budget figures for individual programs. Through September and October the agencies and departments submit their detailed budgets to the OMB.

The OMB and Congress, "as guardians of the public purse... are expected to be more economy-minded than agency heads, who are responsible for the execution of specific programs," two experts have written. They add that on the other hand "agencies or departments rarely ask for all they feel they could use" because this might invite deep cuts and "set a precedent for the future."[24] Hence the agencies cannot aim too high or too low.

The OMB examiner looks at their proposals, and a week or two later a hearing is held at which the agency can make a presentation and the examiner has the chance to question their requests. Once the hearings have finished, the examiner and his supervisors come up with recommendations for the OMB director. Then begins a series of meetings from mid-October to December known as "director's review," in which the examiners present to the director and policy officials their own recommendations

[24] David J. Ott and Attiat F. Ott, *Federal Budget Policy* (Brookings Institution, 1965), p. 20.

139

along with those made by the department or agency. The director then makes his recommendations to the President. Although presidential decisions are final, critical issues can still be appealed until the last minute by cabinet members or agency officials.

Actions Against Impoundment, Backdoor Spending

Large amounts of federal spending in any year are unaffected by congressional action in that year. For some items of expenditure, budget authority is granted, obligations are incurred and outlays made all within one fiscal year. This is the case with the federal payroll, which amounts to nearly one-fifth of total outlays. For many items, however, outlays in any year may stem from budget authority voted in previous years. According to the Brookings Institution's study of the 1975 budget, in recent years about 40 per cent of the outlays, excluding the federal payroll, derived from budget authority of previous years.

On the other hand, authorized funds sometimes go unspent. Congress in 1951 gave the Budget Bureau extensive authority to withhold funds from an agency after they had been appropriated. This device promotes central control over the timing and direction of government spending and helps to prevent an agency from spending faster than Congress intended. But it can also be used to impede a program that is popular with Congress but not with the White House.

During the Nixon presidency, this "impoundment" of appropriated funds became a heated political issue. What upset critics of Nixon's impoundment policy was that it appeared to be directed toward a shift in government social policy, thus circumventing the will of Congress.[25] There were expressions of fear in Congress that impoundment would be used to build up a new form of executive absolutism.

In the last half of 1972 Nixon intensified efforts to induce Congress to conform to his spending plans. When it refused, he vetoed a series of measures authorizing funds for social programs and threatened to withhold the funds if his vetoes were overridden. With the opening of the 93rd Congress in 1973, the struggle between Congress and the White House over impoundment continued. The issue was never resolved so much as it faded from view as Nixon's political strength drained away during his final months in office. By early 1974, Roy Ash declared "We have no impoundment policy."[26] Though his statement was challenged, it was soon apparent that the impoundment policy had become a casualty of Wategate.

[25] See "Presidential Accountability," *E.R.R.*, 1973 Vol. I, pp. 167-184, and "Future of Social Programs," *E.R.R.*, 1973 Vol. I, pp. 251-268.

[26] See *Congressional Quarterly Weekly Report*, March 2, 1974, p. 569.

Congress wrote provisions to prevent impoundment in its Budget Reform Act of 1974 *(see below)*. For impoundments that merely defer spending, Congress can now force the President to release funds if either the House or the Senate passes a resolution calling for their expenditure. For impoundments that terminate programs or cut total spending for fiscal-policy reasons, the law requires that if both the House and Senate do not pass a bill rescinding the appropriation within 45 days, the President must spend the money. To keep Congress informed of impoundment actions the President is required to report deferrals and request rescissions, and the comptroller general can report impoundments if he finds that the President has not.

In another provision of the new law, Congress established procedures to limit "backdoor" spending—spending removed from the control of the Appropriations Committees. In some circumstances, federal officials could enter into contracts obligating federal funds before the money was appropriated, or borrow money before appropriations were made to repay it. The new law, which will come fully into effect in 1976, requires annual appropriations of funds for spending from new contract authority or borrowing authority programs.

Future of Fiscal Reforms in Congress

THE BUDGET REFORM ACT of 1974 is intended to change the fragmentary nature of existing budget procedures, under which Congress considers each revenue and expenditure item separately, taking piecemeal action on spending requests without regard to their overall impact on the budget and the economy. Samuel M. Cohn, a former assistant director of the OMB, said: "For the first time, if it works, we'll be able to see that Congress has to reconcile its action on the totals with its action on the pieces."[27] To give Congress more perspective on the impact of budgetary decisions, the reform act establishes a 23-member House Budget Committee and a 15-member Senate Budget Committee, each of which will have its own staff of around 40 experts.

The House unit appointed Mrs. Nancy Teeters, top budget specialist at the Congressional Research Service in the Library of Congress, to head its economic analysis staff; her counterpart in the Senate unit will be Arnold Packer of the Committee for

---

[27] Quoted in *Congressional Quarterly Weekly Report*, Sept. 7, 1974, p. 2415.

Economic Development, a group whose membership embraces the summit of American business. The key appointment, however, will be a director of the new Congressional Budget Office (CBO), which will provide computers and a staff of some 100 professionals to give Congress the budget analysis capability it previously lacked. The CBO will make its resources available to all congressional committees and members, but will give priority to work for the House and Senate Budget Committees. Its director, who will have a four-year term, could become as influential as the OMB director is in the executive branch. The budget committees and congressional leaders reportedly are looking for a well-known and experienced budget expert such as Kermit Gordon or Charles L. Schultze, who both served as budget directors under President Johnson and moved on to the Brookings Institution.

"...Congress couldn't effectively argue about OMB's measure if it didn't get a yardstick of its own."

Rep. Barber B. Conable Jr. (R N.Y.)

To fit the expanded budget-making procedures into the annual congressional sessions, the beginning of the fiscal year will be shifted from July 1 to Oct. 1 starting with fiscal 1977 on Oct. 1, 1976.[28] The new law also sets a detailed timetable for completing congressional action on the necessary legislation before Oct. 1 each year. By Nov. 10 of the preceding year—almost 11 months before the fiscal year-end—the executive branch must submit a "current services budget" projecting the spending required to maintain existing federal programs without policy changes. The Joint Economic Committee will review that budget and submit an evaluation to Congress by Dec. 31. The President will then submit a revised federal budget to Congress around Jan. 20. His proposals will be reviewed by the House and Senate Budget Committees, in conjunction with the CBO and other committees, and they will draw up a resolution outlining a tentative congressional budget.

May 15 will be the deadline for Congress to approve this initial budget resolution, which will set the goals for appropriations,

[28] The three-month transition period between the end of the fiscal 1976 budget, June 30, 1976, and the beginning of fiscal 1977 will be dealt with separately in President Ford's budget message for fiscal 1976.

spending, taxes, the budget surplus or deficit and the federal debt. These sums will guide but not bind Congress in the following months. By mid-September, after finishing action on all appropriations and spending bills, Congress is required to take another overall look at the budget and adopt a second resolution that will either affirm the target set by the initial resolution, and ensure that spending actions fit it, or revise the target sum.

Expected Difficulties of Making New Plan Work

In order for the new plan to work, legislators and the various committees will have to discipline their actions to the budget timetable. "If they ask for an extension here and an extension there, we could end up with the whole timetable collapsing," warned Sen. Edmund S. Muskie (D Maine), chairman of the Senate Budget Committee. Muskie and his counterpart on the House Budget Committee, Rep. Al Ullman, will also have to guard against attempts to violate or revise the expenditure ceiling.

Although the reforms were designed to control federal spending in the face of inflation, they will undergo their first test in a trial run on the fiscal 1976 budget, at a time when there is pressure to increase federal spending to stimulate the economy. Such spending pressures come on top of the most fundamental obstacle to congressional budget control: the pressure on members of Congress to support federal funds for their districts or states. "There are a lot of guys who voted for this thing who don't really believe in it," a House staff member has said. To make the new system work, Samuel Cohn observed, "Congress and its individual members will have to act a hell of a lot differently than they do now."

The House and Senate Budget Committees are likely to find themselves in conflict with other congressional committees—especially the Appropriations Committees—when they try to fix a spending ceiling. Inevitably the Budget Committee will have to make priority judgments which will threaten some programs and their supporters. "Everyone's prerogatives and powers are involved," Muskie has said. He has taken the major step of leaving the prestigious Senate Foreign Relations Committee to concentrate on his budget job. The Budget Committees' chances for success were enhanced by the resignation of Rep. Wilbur D. Mills (D Ark.) as chairman of the House Ways and Means Committee—making Ullman chairman of both Ways and Means and the House Budget Committee—and by reforms voted by the House Democrats in December 1974 aimed at strengthening their elected leadership at the expense of committee chairmen.

While the long-term budgetary and economic projections of the CBO are regarded as a step in the right direction, a group of Brookings' analysts maintain that they will not go far enough: "...They do not force Congress to deal explicitly with such questions as what programs should be cut in 1978 if Congress votes now for a program entailing sizable expenditures in 1978. Real improvement here can only come from procedures that require Congress to vote on budgetary measures more in advance of the actual spending, when there is still time to reduce other appropriations to provide the requisite budgetary flexibility."[29]

Criticism of 'Tax Expenditures'; Reform Demands

Despite its measures to reform budgeting procedures, the 93rd Congress took no action in another area of fiscal control where there is mounting controversy—the nation's tax laws. Two years of study by the House Ways and Means Committee resulted in three separate tax-revision bills, none of which was sent to the House floor. At a time when the budget is being scrutinized for every possible saving, there is increasing dissatisfaction with the federal government's "tax expenditures"—revenues that the government fails to collect because tax laws shield some forms of gain in wealth from the normal application of the federal income tax.

Stanley S. Surrey, a former Treasury official long interested in tax reform, wrote in a recent book analyzing tax expenditures, "It can generally be said that less critical analysis is paid to these tax expenditures than to almost any direct expenditure program."[30]

Tax Analysts and Advocates, a private tax research group, has estimated that federal "tax expenditures" for fiscal 1975 will total some $78.3 billion.[31] Yet these expenditures represent a very different set of priorities than those embodied in the outlay budget. Samuel Hastings-Black, a tax attorney for the group, testified Feb. 15, 1974, before the Joint Economic Committee that because of tax incentives for business and investment activities, "the annual federal effort is significantly more oriented toward business enterprise...than would appear" from the government's budget documents. According to the group's estimates, 38 per cent or about $28 billion of fiscal 1975 tax expenditures will be devoted to capital gains, investments, manufacturing and business, mining, timber and oil.

---

[29] Blechman et al., *op. cit.*, p. 266.

[30] Stanley S. Surrey, *Pathways to Tax Reform: The Concept of Tax Expenditures* (1973), p. 6. Surrey, a Harvard Law School professor, served as Assistant Secretary of the Treasury in the Johnson administration.

[31] Tax Analysts and Advocates, "Fiscal Year 1975 Tax Expenditure Budget," *Tax Notes*, Jan. 21, 1974, pp. 4-19.

Surrey and others contend that tax expenditures inhibit the fair operation of a progressive income tax that was intended to tax most heavily those most able to pay. While tax expenditures do help the poor as well as the wealthy, Surrey suggests that their benefits at low-income levels are largely confined to the elderly. Critics also charge that allowing deductions from taxable income erodes the overall income base on which taxes are levied, thus forcing the government to maintain high nominal tax rates in order to raise the revenues it needs. The American Bar Association's Special Committee on Substantive Tax Reform, using a "substantially broadened but by no means comprehensive tax base" and eliminating the corporate income tax found that the same tax revenue from both corporate and private incomes could be raised by a flat rate of 14 per cent on personal income alone.[32]

"...The tax expenditure system is the primary source of unfairness in our tax system."

Stanley S. Surrey
Former Treasury official

Through budgetary reform and the examination of tax expenditures, the federal government can establish an increasingly coherent fiscal policy. In the short run, the federal budget is difficult to change, especially because of the growing proportion of uncontrollable expenditures. In the longer run, however, policy changes can have a great effect on the budget. Difficult budgetary choices will still have to be made, for new demands for federal spending must be dealt with out of limited fiscal resources. The energy crisis calls for a fiscal policy to encourage the efficient use of existing fuel resources while also aiding the development of new forms of energy. Fiscal action could take the form of direct grants for research and development, tax incentives to producers, or support for mass transit construction.

If present expenditures and tax rates are maintained, the Brookings study of the 1975 budget calculated, and prices rise at the rate of 3 per cent between 1975 and 1980, revenues will exceed expenditures by $72 billion in fiscal 1980. If inflation is greater, the surplus will be even larger. But new demands on federal funds are certain to grow. Thus the necessity to increase

---

[32] Quoted by Warren L. Coats Jr., "The Principles of Tax Reform," *Challenge,* January-February 1974, p. 21.

funds available to finance new programs, either through cutbacks or tax reforms, and to resist the temptation to enter into
new programs without understanding their long-term fiscal implications, are as important as ever.

Selected Bibliography

Books

Blechman, Barry M., et. al., *Setting National Priorities: The 1975
    Budget*, The Brookings Institution, 1974.
Congress and the Nation, Vol. III, Congressional Quarterly Inc., 1973.
Congressional Quarterly's Guide to the Congress of the United States,
    Congressional Quarterly Inc., 1971.
Inflation and Unemployment, Congressional Quarterly Inc., 1975.
Okun, Arthur M., *The Political Economy of Prosperity*, The Brook-
    ings Institution, 1970.
Surrey, Stanley S., *Pathways to Tax Reform: The Concept of Tax Ex-
    penditures*, Harvard University Press, 1973.

Articles

Coats, Warren L. Jr., "The Principles of Tax Reform," *Challenge*,
    January-February 1974.
Conable, Barber B. Jr., "Making Congressional Sense of the Budget,"
    Ripon Forum, January 1974.
"How to Fight Inflation and Recession," *Business Week*, Dec. 7, 1974.
"Inflation and the Budgetary Outlook," *The Brookings Bulletin*,
    spring 1974.
"Investment Outlook 1975: Washington Forecast," *Business Week*,
    Dec. 21, 1974.
"A Stunning Decline, a Long Road Back," *Fortune*, January 1975.
Tax Analysts and Advocates, "Fiscal Year 1975 Tax Expenditure Bud-
    get," *Tax Notes*, Jan. 21, 1974.
Odeen, Philip, "In Defense of the Defense Budget," *Foreign Policy*,
    fall 1974.

Reports and Studies

The Budget of the United States Government, Fiscal Year 1975,
    U.S. Government Printing Office, 1974.
Editorial Research Reports, "Limits On Federal Spending," 1972 Vol.
    II, p. 889; "Future of Social Programs," 1973 Vol. I, p. 249; "Fed-
    eral Budget Making," 1969 Vol. I, p. 1; "Peacetime Defense
    Spending," 1974 Vol. I, p. 261.
Joint Economic Committee, Congress of the United States, "Achieving
    Price Stability Through Economic Growth," Dec. 29, 1974.
——"The 1976 Current Services Budget: A Staff Study," Dec. 31, 1974.

Antitrust Action

by

Suzanne de Lesseps

1 9 7 5
Jan. 31

ANTITRUST ACTION

A RECENT WAVE of antitrust lawsuits brought by the Justice Department has caused a stir in the nation's business and legal communities. Many are asking if the government is indeed determined to open an era of tough enforcement. President Ford has said antitrust action is a weapon in his administration's fight against inflation, and a spate of legal moves indicates that his words are to be taken seriously. Still, the history of antitrust activity has been marked by peaks and valleys of interest and enforcement. The peaks dwindle into valleys as investigation and litigation drag on for years or the political climate changes.

It is a bit of political folklore in Washington that a Republican in the White House is likely to insist on strict enforcement of antitrust laws to dispel his party's pro-business image among the electorate. The truth or falsity of this notion is subject to argument but it apparently is held strongly enough to give American business added concern about the present state of economic affairs.

"I am determined to return to the vigorous enforcement of antitrust laws," President Ford told Congress on Oct. 8 in a message on inflation. Price-fixing and bid-rigging were two violations which, he said, would be prosecuted "to the full extent of the law." In addition, Ford requested that the lawmakers raise the maximum penalty in antitrust criminal cases from one year's imprisonment to three and in civil cases raise the limit on fines to $1 million for corporations and $100,000 for individuals. The ceiling on both penalties had been $50,000 since 1955. Congress complied with his request in a bill—the Antitrust Procedures and Penalties Act—passed on Dec. 11 and signed into law ten days later.

In a further indication of the new mood in Washington, Attorney General William B. Saxbe on Oct. 29 told the Legal Committee of the Grocery Manufacturers of America that "the vigorous and impartial enforcement of the antitrust laws is a top priority in the Department of Justice." In a speech to the National Association of Manufacturers in December, Saxbe named specific areas being investigated for price-fixing violations.[1] Saxbe has since resigned[2] and the man Ford has nominated to succeed him, Edward H. Levi, told the Senate Judiciary Committee at his confirmation hearing on Jan. 28 that the government should look into energy industries for possible antitrust violations that hold back production or illegally boost prices. Levi, currently president of the University of Chicago, held posts in the Justice Department during World War II, including that of first assistant in the antitrust division in 1944-45.

In an end-of-the-year report, the Justice Department reported that 33 criminal indictments had been returned against antitrust violators during 1974, the highest number since 1962, and that 38 civil antitrust cases had been filed. A major case filed on Nov. 20 charged the American Telephone & Telegraph Co. (AT&T) with illegally monopolizing the telecommunications industry and sought the divestiture of the company's large manufacturing subsidiary, the Western Electric Co. Another corporate giant, the International Business Machines (IBM) is scheduled to go on trial Feb. 18 on long-pending[3] charges of monopolizing the computer industry and manipulating prices.

Justice Department's Attempt to Break Up AT&T

In terms of assets, the American Telephone & Telegraph Co. is the largest corporation in the United States. At the end of 1973, its assets were $67 billion, and its profits totaled almost $3 billion that year. The company employs over one million persons and has approximately three million stockholders, more than any other company. Through its 23 regional telephone companies, AT&T owns and services 112 million telephones, about 80 per cent of the nation's total. The remaining 20 per cent are served by 1,700 smaller, independent companies.

As a regulated, public service monopoly, AT&T has exclusive franchises for local-exchange telephone service in various parts of the country. The government antitrust suit does not challenge this domination of local operations. It does, however, charge the company with monopolizing telephone-equipment manufacturing and long-distance operations by refusing to allow competitive companies to hook non-Bell equipment into the Bell System network.

AT&T buys almost all of its telecommunications equipment from Western Electric, which is not regulated by the

---

[1] He mentioned the pricing of beef, eggs, dairy products, seafood, beer, soft drinks, and wholesale groceries generally. He also said investigations would extend to such self-regulated or state-regulated professions as medicine, pharmacy, accounting, engineering and veterinary science.

[2] Saxbe resigned Dec. 13 and was confirmed Dec. 19 by the Senate as ambassador to India but continued temporarily in his old job. Ford nominated Levi on Jan. 14.

[3] The suit was filed Jan. 17, 1969, the last working day of the Johnson administration.

The Bell Telephone System

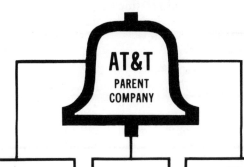

AT&T
PARENT
COMPANY

WESTERN ELECTRIC COMPANY
(wholly owned manufacturing subsidiary)

LONG LINES DEPT.

BELL LABORATORIES
(owned jointly by parent company and Western Electric)

ASSOCIATED COMPANIES

(percent of AT&T ownership in parentheses)

New England Telephone & Telegraph Co. (85.4)
The Southern New England Telephone Co. (16.8)
New York Telephone Co. (100)
New Jersey Bell Telephone Co. (100)
The Bell Telephone Co. of Pennsylvania (100)
The Chesapeake & Potomac Telephone Co. (D.C.)(100)
The Chesapeake & Potomac Telephone Co. of Maryland (100)
The Chesapeake & Potomac Telephone Co. of Virginia (100)
The Chesapeake & Potomac Telephone Co. of West Virginia (100)
Southern Bell Telephone & Telegraph Co. (100)
South Central Bell Telephone Co. (100)
The Ohio Bell Telephone Co. (100)
Cincinnati Bell Inc. (25.7)
Michigan Bell Telephone Co. (100)
Indiana Bell Telephone Co., Inc. (100)
Wisconsin Telephone Co. (100)
Illinois Bell Telephone Co. (100)
Northwestern Bell Telephone Co. (100)
Southwestern Bell Telephone Co. (100)
The Mountain States Telephone & Telegraph Co. (87.8)
Pacific Northwest Bell Telephone Co. (89.3)
The Pacific Telephone & Telegraph Co. (89.8)
Bell Canada (2.0)

government. The company's telephone rates are computed on the basis of what regulatory agencies determine will yield a fair rate of return. These computations are based on operating costs. Since operating costs include equipment, an unregulated expense, the government suspects that telephone rates may be higher than necessary.

AT&T denies that telephone rates are too high, and it contends that Western Electric is able to produce equipment at low prices because of the manufacturing company's immense size. If forced to relinquish its manufacturing subsidiary, AT&T argues, the Bell System will be forced to pay higher prices for equipment. The government replies that independents provide reasonable rates without buying low-priced equipment from a subsidiary.

The Justice Department also seeks to separate AT&T's Long Lines department from the 23 regional Bell companies. The Long Lines unit operates all interstate communication lines and is responsible for 90 per cent of all long distance calls in the United States. While the department does not actually operate telephones, it provides the facilities needed to connect the lines of Bell companies and independents to form a long distance network. If AT&T were separated from its Long Lines unit, independent companies would gain a larger share of long distance revenues. AT&T argues, on the other hand, that the Long Lines department helps subsidize lower local rates, and if its revenues were lost, Bell customer rates would rise.

Telephone Company's Defense of Its Structure

In a statement issued immediately after the suit was filed, AT&T Chairman John D. deButts defended his company's structure. "The telephone network to work efficiently must be designed, built and operated as a single entity," he said. DeButts further warned that the government suit "could lead to fragmentation of responsibility for the nation's telephone network. If that happens, telephone service would deteriorate and cost much, much more." DeButts indicated that AT&T would consider the cost of the suit to the company when it asked for future rate increases.[4]

Moreover, AT&T contends that it is protected from new antitrust action as a result of a similar suit which was settled out of court in 1956. The settlement in that case, which had begun seven years earlier, allowed the company to retain Western Electric. It was later disclosed that the settlement was arranged by Herbert Brownell, attorney general in the Eisenhower ad-

---

[4] On Jan. 3, AT&T filed a proposal with the Federal Communications Commission for an average 7.2 per cent increase in long-distance rates. The company cited inflation and increased construction costs as the chief reasons for the requested increase. No official mention was made of the cost of the antitrust suit.

ministration, and T. Brooke Price, AT&T general counsel. Keith I. Clearwaters, deputy assistant attorney general of the Justice Department's antitrust division, retorts that some of the communications services which AT&T is now accused of monopolizing, such as microwave communications, did not exist in 1956.

Issues Surrounding the IBM Monopoly Case

Like the suit against AT&T, the suit against IBM takes on enormous significance because of the defending company's immense size. IBM is the undisputed king of the computer industry. In 1974, its sales totaled $12.7 billion and its net income reached $1.8 billion. In terms of its 1973 sales, which totaled $11 billion, IBM ranked tenth on *Fortune* magazine's list of the 50 largest industrial companies in the world that year.[5] Judge David N. Edelstein, who will preside at the trial in U.S. District Court in New York City, has remarked that the case's "potential impact and consequences involve not only the data processing industry but such things as relations with foreign governments and the balance of trade. It's not like A suing B. This case involves the world and the public."[6]

The government has charged IBM with monopolizing the computer industry through price manipulation and illegal marketing procedures. Justice said one way in which IBM monopolized the market was by selling all elements of a computer system under a fixed price. This includes hardware, programing and peripheral equipment such as tape and disc storage devices. IBM'S competitors have long complained about its domination of the computer market.

International Data Corporation, a research organization which surveys the computer industry regularly, estimated that at the end of 1973 the value of computers in use throughout the world amounted to $44.5 billion and that 60 per cent of the equipment was manufactured by IBM.

The Justice Department seeks "major structural relief" in its suit against IBM, although without specifically indicating how the company should be broken up. It is generally believed that the department will seek to separate IBM into five or six independent and competitive organizations. James Ensor of the London *Financial Times* reported Nov. 20 that Justice had considered the possibility of creating each separate company around a specific IBM product, such as printers, memory banks, central processors, "software" (programing) and office

---

[5] *Fortune,* August 1974, p. 185.
[6] Quoted in "Bigness Under Attack: The U.S. vs. IBM," *Business Week,* Nov. 11, 1972, pp. 110-111.

products. Since this might lead to problems of collusion between the new companies, Ensor suggested that officials at Justice would probably want the companies organized around IBM plants.

IBM's smaller competitors are reported to have mixed feelings about splitting the company into independent units. Several are said to fear that competition would become chaotic, and the U.S. computer industry would lose its prestige in the world market. *Forbes* magazine quoted Ray Macdonald, chairman of the Burroughs Corp., as saying that he can compete with one IBM, but the existence of four or five IBM's would tend to "increase rather than decrease" the share of market sales for the IBM companies.[7] If six new companies of equal size were created out of IBM, each would be larger than either of IBM's biggest competitors, Sperry Univac or Honeywell.

On Jan. 24, the Tenth U.S. Circuit Court of Appeals in Denver reversed a lower court decision which had ordered IBM to pay $259.5 million in antitrust damages to the Telex Corp., a supplier of computer equipment. The trial court in Dallas in September 1973 had found IBM guilty of predatory pricing and other violations of the Sherman Antitrust Act. *The Wall Street Journal* commented Jan. 27: "The new ruling in IBM's favor is expected to have a profound impact on the many other civil antitrust suits outstanding against IBM. Chief among these is the Justice Department's six-year-old complaint..." Telex is expected to appeal to the Supreme Court.

Development of U.S. Antitrust Laws

DURING THE second half of the 19th century, following the Civil War, the United States underwent a period of vast industrial growth and concentration. Historians Allan Nevins and Henry Steele Commager cite four reasons for this development: First of all, the expansion of the railroads linked the country together, opening the West and providing a national market for manufactured products.

Second, patent laws encouraged monopolies by giving one manufacturer total control over important tools and mechanical processes. Third, the government's liberal interpretation of land laws and its generous land grants encouraged companies to develop and exploit the nation's minerals and timber. Finally, a

---

[7] "More For The Parts Than The Whole," *Forbes*, Sept. 1, 1974, p. 28.

company was able to incorporate in a state with loose regulatory laws and do business in other states where the laws were more restrictive.[8]

Standard Oil as Creator of the Trust Movement

The forerunner of the trust system, a system known as "pooling," sprang up in the 1870s as a means of surviving the tough competition of that period. Pooling has been described as a gentlemen's agreement between rival producers or railroad directors to maintain prices and divide business. The first formally recognized trust appeared in 1882, the creation of Standard Oil lawyer Samuel Dodd. Since Standard Oil's articles of incorporation did not authorize it to hold stock in other companies or to be a partner in any firm, Dodd had the company buy stock not in the name of Standard Oil but in the name of a trustee.

"If we will not endure a king as a political power, we will not endure a king over production, transportation, and sale of any of the necessaries of life."

Sen. John Sherman in 1890

This arrangement was embodied in the Standard Oil Trust Agreement, drawn up on Jan. 2, 1882. All stock and properties, including those of Standard Oil itself as well as those outside of Ohio, the state of incorporation, were transferred to a board of trustees. The board consisted of the principal owners and managers, with John D. Rockefeller at its head. The trust agreement called for the formation of a Standard Oil company in every state or federal territory, but this plan was never fulfilled. Companies were organized, however, in New York, New Jersey, Kentucky, Indiana, Kansas, Nebraska and California.

Following Standard Oil's example, approximately 5,000 industrial businesses merged into about 300 trusts or corporations in the 1880s and 1890s. A cottonseed oil trust appeared in 1884 and a linseed oil trust one year later. The lead trust, the whiskey trust and the sugar trust all emerged in 1887 and were followed by the match trust in 1889, the tobacco trust in 1890 and the rubber trust in 1892. By 1900, 185 industrial combinations were turning out 14 per cent of the country's industrial products. In

---

[8] Nevins and Commager, *A Pocket History of the United States* (1956), p. 276.

1901, eight separate companies including the Carnegie Steel Company, merged to form U.S. Steel—the first billion-dollar corporation in the United States.

The merger was primarily financed by J. Pierpont Morgan, creator of one of the most powerful trusts of the period—the famous "money trust." Through his control of the banking business, Morgan was able to influence many sectors of the American economy, including manufacturing, mining, insurance companies, utilities, shipping lines and communication systems. He helped to organize and refinance many railroad companies, and after the panic of 1893, the House of Morgan controlled a dozen major lines.

Sherman Act and Turn-of-Century Reform Era

Richard Hofstadter has said the "structure of business... became the object of a widespread hostility which stemmed from the feeling that business was becoming a closed system of authoritative action."[9] Americans soon began to demand that government take action to reform the powerful influence of the trusts.

Congress responded by passing the Sherman Antitrust Act in 1890. "If we will not endure a king as a political power, we should not endure a king over production, transportation, and sale of any of the necessaries of life," said Sen. John Sherman (R Ohio), one of the leading sponsors of the act.[10] The Sherman Act barred "every contract, combination...or conspiracy in restraint of trade" as well as actions that "monopolize or attempt to monopolize...any part of the trade," both domestic and foreign. Any violation of the act constituted a criminal offense punishable by fine or prison sentence, or sometimes both.

In the beginning it looked as though the Sherman Act was going to be virtually meaningless. The Supreme Court dismissed a government suit against the whiskey trust and shortly afterward dropped a case against the cash register trust. In 1895, the Court ruled that although the sugar trust had acquired control of 98 per cent of the sugar refined in the United States, this did not in itself constitute "restraint of trade." The making of sugar was what was being monopolized, the Court ruled, but not the interstate trade and commerce of the product.[11]

When Theodore Roosevelt became President in 1901, public hostility toward the trusts was being further aroused by a group of writers who came to be known as muckrakers. Lincoln Steffens, for example, while an editor successively at *McClure's*,

---

[9] Richard Hofstadter, *The Age of Reform* (1955), p. 229.
[10] Quoted by A.D. Neal in *The Antitrust Laws of the U.S.A.* (1962), p. 25.
[11] United States *v.* E.C. Knight Co., 156 U.S. 1 (1895).

American and *Everybody's* magazines, published a series of biting commentaries on municipal corruption and boss rule in the cities.[12] These were collected in *The Shame of the Cities* (1904), *Upbuilders* (1909) and other books. Upton Sinclair attacked the meat packing industry in a novel, *The Jungle* (1906), and Ida M. Tarbell attacked the abuses of the oil industry in her *History of the Standard Oil Company* (1904).

In 1903 the antitrust division was established in the Justice Department with William A. Day at its head. The division consisted of six lawyers and four stenographers. Roosevelt himself took up the "trust-busting" crusade, saying: "As far as the antitrust laws go, they will be enforced, and when suit is undertaken it will not be compromised except on the basis that the government wins."[13]

Early Supreme Court Rulings in Antitrust Cases

The Northern Securities case in 1904 strengthened the Sherman Act and marked the beginning of a new era. The Supreme Court ruled that the Northern Securities Co., which had been formed to hold the stock of the competing Great Northern and Northern Pacific railroads, had been used as an illegal device in restraint of trade.[14] In 1911, the Supreme Court ordered the breakup of the American Tobacco Co. and the Standard Oil Co.

Nineteen years earlier, in 1892, Standard Oil had reorganized as a holding company in New Jersey to escape action taken against it by the Ohio Supreme Court. The U.S. Supreme Court, however, dissolved the holding company and prohibited the Standard Oil Co. of New Jersey from exerting any control over its 33 subsidiaries. The divestment resulted in the creation of 34 independent companies. Altogether, the government brought legal action against 44 trusts during the Theodore Roosevelt administration and 90 more under President Taft.

In 1914, Congress responded to President Wilson's requests for additional antitrust legislation by passing the Clayton Antitrust Act and the Federal Trade Commission Act. The Clayton Act, drafted by Rep. Henry De Lamar Clayton (D Ala.), contained prohibitions against price discrimination, exclusive sales contracts, interlocking directorates and the acquisition of capital stock interests in a competitor. Peaceful strikes, picketing and

---

[12] Roosevelt chose the occasion of dedicating an office building of the House of Representatives, April 14, 1906, to denounce reform journalists for attacking the character of Chauncey M. Depew, a railroad magnate. He called them "muckrakers" on the basis of a passage in John Bunyan's *Pilgrim's Progress*. The new word was adopted by defenders and critics of the reform movement.

[13] Quoted by Nevins and Commager, *op. cit.*, p. 285.

[14] Northern Securities Co. *v.* United States, 193 U.S. 197 (1904).

boycotts were declared legal and the use of the court injunction against labor was restricted.

The Federal Trade Commission Act established the FTC and gave it power to issue cease-and-desist orders against corporations in violation of the Clayton Act and to report antitrust violations to the attorney general. The commission was composed of members appointed by the President for seven-year terms. As amended in 1938, the Federal Trade Commission Act outlaws "unfair methods of competition in commerce and unfair or deceptive acts...in commerce."

Change in Political Climate After World War I

By 1920, the climate of opinion toward big business had changed. That year, the Supreme Court refused to dissolve the United States Steel Corp. even though it controlled more than 50 per cent of the country's steel output.[15] This decision contributed to a new wave of industrial mergers. In 1926 the Court weakened the Clayton Act by holding that in the case of a corporation acquiring the stock of another company, the FTC was without power to prevent the merger if the corporation had exchanged the stock for the physical assets of the acquired company before the commission issued a cease-and-desist order.[16] During the five-year period from 1925 to 1930, more than 1,238 consolidations occurred resulting in the disappearance of almost 7,000 companies. The prosperous Twenties, however, came to an end with the crash of the stock market in October 1929 and the onset of the depression.

During the early years of the depression, the antitrust laws were virtually suspended. The National Industrial Recovery Act of 1933, a foundation stone of Franklin D. Roosevelt's "New Deal," permitted trade associations and other industrial groups to control prices and production. These groups were exempted from prosecution under the antitrust laws by the use of so-called codes of fair competition. More than 400 of these codes were filed with the National Recovery Administration during the first month of its existence. Many of the codes were approved hastily and code groups were allowed to do many things the antitrust laws forbade. Consequently, in 1935, the Supreme Court ruled the codes and the act unconstitutional.

Toward the end of the decade, the staff and budget at the Justice Department's antitrust division and the FTC were enlarged. In 1938, Roosevelt asked Congress for a full investigation of industry concentrations in an effort to determine if the

---

[15] United States v. United States Steel Corp., 251 U.S. 417 (1920).
[16] FTC v. Western Meat Co., Thatcher Mfg. Co. v. FTC, Swift & Co. v. FTC, 272 U.S. 554 (1926).

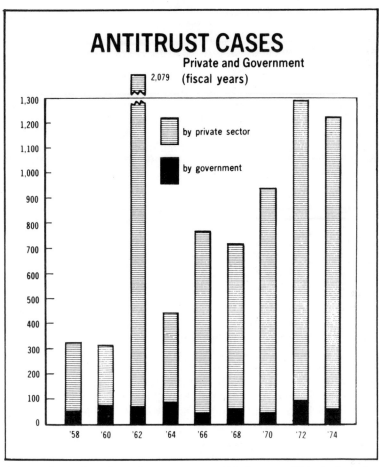

ANTITRUST CASES
Private and Government
(fiscal years)

2,079

by private sector

by government

1,300
1,200
1,100
1,000
900
800
700
600
500
400
300
200
100
0

'58 '60 '62 '64 '66 '68 '70 '72 '74

depression related to the structure of industry. This led to the creation of a Temporary National Economic Committee, composed of three U.S. senators, three U.S. representatives, and one delegate each from the Securities and Exchange Commission and the departments of Labor, Treasury and Commerce. The committee was unable to link the country's economic woes to industry mergers, but its hearings helped spark a new interest in antitrust legislation.

Enforcement Through 1960s; GE Price-Fixing

A revival of strict antitrust enforcement emerged in 1938 under the leadership of Thurman Arnold, head of the antitrust division at Justice. Under Arnold's direction, the division expanded and promptly opened a nationwide investigation of the building industry. In 1940, the Justice Department filed more antitrust cases than had been filed in the 20 years after the passage of the Sherman Act. Before Arnold left the department in 1943, it had brought 230 lawsuits against business and labor monopolies. Despite this activity, 1940-47 was still a period of industrial combinations; some 2,000 mergers took place during those years.

Because of this increasing trend in concentration, President Truman urged Congress to carry out a new study of monopoly power in the United States. That study led to the passage of the Celler-Kefauver Act in 1950, which strengthened the Clayton Act by prohibiting mergers through acquisition of assets. Between 1951 and 1964, over 140 mergers were challenged by the Justice Department and the Federal Trade Commission.

In 1961, 29 manufacturing firms and 44 of their officials were convicted of bid-rigging and price-fixing in the sale of heavy electrical equipment during 1955-59. Seven executives, including two vice presidents and the general manager of General Electric, were sentenced to 30 days in prison for violation of antitrust laws. A total of $1,924,500 in fines was levied against the defendant corporations and officials in the case.[17]

Several Supreme Court decisions in the 1960s served to strengthen antitrust enforcement. In 1962, for example, the Court ruled that the combination of Brown Shoe Co. and G. R. Kinney Co. was illegal, even though the two companies combined controlled less than 5 per cent of the country's shoe production and less than 2.5 per cent of all retail shoe outlets.[18] In U.S. *v.* Philadelphia National Bank, the Court ruled in 1963 that the Clayton Act applied to commercial bank consolidations.[19] And in 1967, the Court established that it was illegal for a manufacturer to restrict a wholesaler's rights to sell goods which were purchased from the manufacturer.[20]

Problems of Federal Enforcement

THE JUSTICE DEPARTMENT and the Federal Trade Commission share the major responsibility for the enforcement of the nation's antitrust laws. Only the Justice Department has the authority to bring criminal proceedings against antitrust violators. The Federal Trade Commission Act of 1914 gives the FTC broad civil authority and allows it to investigate business practices that are collusive or that violate fair trade practices.

---

[17] For details of the case, see Richard Austin Smith, "The Incredible Electrical Conspiracy," in two parts, *Fortune*, April 1961, pp. 132-137, 170-180; May 1961, pp. 161-164, 210-224.

[18] Brown Shoe Co. *v.* United States, 370 U.S. 294 (1962).

[19] 274 U.S. 321 (1963).

[20] U.S. *v.* Arnold, Schwinn & Co., 388 U.S. 365.

Ralph Nader and a number of others have said that antitrust laws were not being vigorously enforced. "...Antitrust division chiefs lack the resources and vigor to file against the many violations which occur, and they lack the courage and creativity to formulate new cases to cope with new problems," stated a 1972 Nader task force report on antitrust enforcement titled *The Closed Enterprise System.* At hearings held in November 1974 by the congressional Joint Economic Committee on the FTC's role in combating inflation, Sen. William Proxmire (D Wis.) said: "A real antitrust, decentralization, pro-competition economic policy has never been seriously pursued, and is not now being pursued. There has been a lot of lip service to the goal of competitive free enterprise...[but] there has been little performance as far as policy makers and higher government officials are concerned."[21]

View That Regulatory Agencies Stifle Competition

The federal regulatory agencies are charged with protecting the public interest in such areas as transportation, communications, electrical energy and securities exchange. In all, the federally regulated sectors of the economy account for more than 10 per cent of the gross national product. The agencies have been accused of serving the industries they regulate better than the public.[22] They have been specifically accused of stifling competition through rate-fixing and licensing.

Assistant Attorney General Thomas E. Kauper, head of the antitrust division, has said that "much of this regulation, frequently justified by reference to natural monopoly and 'ruinous' competition, has contributed substantially to the pressures of inflation." "Heavily regulated industries," he continues, "are relatively unresponsive to consumer needs, which must be translated through a bureaucratic intermediary."[23] The chairman of the Federal Trade Commission, Lewis A. Engman, has had this to say: "Much of today's regulatory machinery does little more than shelter producers from the normal competitive consequences of lassitude and inefficiency. Most regulated industries have become federal protectorates living in a cozy world of cost-plus, safely protected from the ugly specters of competition and innovation."[24]

The Civil Aeronautics Board, Engman complained, overregulates the airline industry to the extent that "there is no

---

[21] See *Congressional Quarterly Weekly Report,* Nov. 30, 1974, p. 3217.
[22] See "Federal Regulatory Agencies: Fourth Branch of Government," *E.R.R.,* 1969 Vol. I, pp. 85-102.
[23] Speech before the Chicago Bar Association's Committee on Antitrust Law and the Illinois State Bar Association Section on Antitrust Law, in Chicago, Oct. 31, 1974.
[24] Quoted in *The New York Times,* Oct. 8, 1974.

Recent Antitrust Action

Oct. 7. A federal grand jury in New York City indicted three leading department stores and two of their top executives on charges of conspiring to fix the prices of women's clothing. The stores were Saks Fifth Avenue, Bergdorf Goodman and Bonwit Teller.

Oct. 31. The Federal Trade Commission issued an antitrust complaint against four major oil companies—Exxon, Amoco, Standard Oil of California and Standard Oil of Ohio—for allegedly conspiring to eliminate competition among themselves in the sale of automobile tires.

Nov. 20. The Justice Department filed a major antitrust case against AT&T *(see p. 150)*

Nov. 25. Justice filed a civil antitrust suit against 21 major American publishers charging them with conspiring to divide the world book market into exclusive territories.

Dec. 10. The Federal Trade Commission issued an intitrust complaint against the Continental Baking Co., a subsidiary of International Telephone & Telegraph Co., accusing them of monopolizing the wholesale market for baked bread.

Justice refiled a civil antitrust suit against the three major commercial television networks, accusing them of monopolizing entertainment programing during prime time. The networks had claimed that similar suits filed in 1972 were the result of President Nixon's displeasure over the television coverage of Watergate. Those suits were dismissed in November 1974.

Dec. 13. Eight major chemical companies, including E.I. duPont de Nemours & Co., were fined a total of $360,500 by a federal district court in New Jersey on charges of illegally fixing the prices of dyes.

Dec. 19. Six sugar refining companies were indicted by a federal grand jury in San Francisco on charges of illegal price fixing.

Dec. 20. A federal district judge in San Francisco ruled that the National Football League's contract and reserve system was a violation of the nation's antitrust laws. The reserve system binds players to one team.

Jan. 21. The FTC filed a complaint against Nestle Alimentana S.A., based in Switzerland, charging that the organization's acquisition of the Stouffer Corp. in 1973 reduces competition in the frozen food market.

---

competition at all" in rates and routing schedules.[25] In October 1974, when the CAB issued guidelines establishing minimum rates for trans-Atlantic charter flights, the Justice Department filed a petition with the agency charging that the guidelines constituted illegal rate fixing.

In the same speech calling for tougher antitrust enforcement, President Ford asked Congress in October 1974 to create a National Commission on Regulatory Reform. It would "identify and eliminate existing federal rules and regulations that increase costs to the consumer without any good reason in today's economic climate." The chairmen of six[26] of the regula-

[25] For a similar view of the CAB's regulation of the airline industry, see K.G.J. Pilai's "The CAB as Travel Regulator," in *The Monopoly Makers* (1971), pp. 159-189.

[26] Federal Trade Commission, Federal Power Commission, Consumer Product Safety Commission, Interstate Commerce Commission, Civil Aeronautics Board and Federal Communications Commission.

tory commissions endorsed the idea in November 1974, but Helen Bentley, chairman of the Federal Maritime Commission, dissented. She said the "expenses of such a commission would be unjustified in the light of the result it would obtain."

The government's ability to zealously enforce antitrust laws is said to be hindered by a lack of money and manpower. *The Washington Post* commented editorially on Nov. 24 that the increase in AT&T's dividend in 1974 was "greater than the antitrust division's budget for the last 10 years combined." The newspaper said that AT&T "can put more resources into defending this lawsuit—without feeling a pinch—than the government is likely to put into its prosecution."

The antitrust division's budget for fiscal year 1974 was $14.8 million, and the budget for 1975 totals $16.8 million—a 14 per cent increase. This increase provided 83 new staff positions, including those for 40 attorneys and seven economists. *The Wall Street Journal* reported on Jan. 14 that a similar increase in staff attorneys was expected in the fiscal 1976 budget. The Federal Trade Commission's budget amounted to $32 million in 1974 and $37.9 million in 1975. The FTC currently employs about 550 attorneys.

As the Justice Department attempts to handle both the IBM and AT&T cases, its antitrust staff will be stretched to capacity. A time-consuming aspect of an antitrust investigation is the "discovery process" during which the government and the defendant examine each other's files. In the IBM case, Justice Department lawyers had to consider five billion records and documents in thousands of files in a company that employs 265,000 persons around the world. It has taken the IBM case six years to reach the trial stage, and analysts estimate that the AT&T case will take eight to ten years. Justice has already filed its first request for documents from AT&T, including all material since Jan. 1, 1930, relating to the purchase of Western Electric equipment by AT&T. It has been estimated that the government and AT&T will exchange tens of millions of papers.

Political Pressures; Nixon's ITT Intervention

The nature of antitrust enforcement is often shaped by the political pressures of the time. An example of these pressures was provided in Watergate-related disclosures concerning the 1971 settlement of an antitrust case against International Telephone and Telegraph Corp. (ITT), a company with no connection to AT&T. In 1969, Justice filed three suits against ITT, charging violation of antitrust laws in its acquisition of the Hartford Fire Insurance Co., the Grinnell Corp. and the Canteen Food Vending Corp. By 1971, the government had lost in the courts and Richard W. McLaren, then head of the antitrust division, was considering an appeal to the Supreme Court.

A House Judiciary Committee transcript of a five-minute White House telephone call on April 19, 1971, showed that President Nixon ordered Richard Kleindienst, who was then deputy attorney general and McLaren's superior, to drop the case. Nixon told Kleindienst: "I want something clearly understood, and if it is not understood, McLaren's ass is to be out within one hour. The ITT thing—stay the hell out of it. Is that clear? That's an order.... I do not want McLaren to run around prosecuting people, raising hell about conglomerates, stirring things up at this point. Now you keep him the hell out of that. Is that clear?"[27]

According to a background paper later issued by the White House to explain its actions in the ITT case, John Mitchell, then the attorney general, advised Nixon on April 21 that it was politically unsound to prohibit the Justice Department from appealing to the Supreme Court. Mitchell was afraid that Solicitor General Erwin N. Griswold might resign in protest and thus embarrass the administration. "Based upon the Attorney General's recommendations," the White House paper explained, "the President reversed his decision of April 19, 1971, and authorized the Department of Justice to proceed with the case...."[28]

Meanwhile, McLaren decided to settle the case by consent decree while the appeal was pending. By the terms of the agreement, ITT was allowed to keep the profitable Hartford Insurance Co. in return for divesting itself of (1) Canteen, (2) the fire protection division of Grinnell, (3) Hamilton Life Insurance Co., (4) Life Insurance Co. of New York, (5) Avis Rent-A-Car and (6) Levitt & Sons construction firm. The annual sales of these

---

[27] Quoted in Book V, Part 1, "Statement of Information, Hearings Before the Committee on the Judiciary," House of Representatives, p. 316 (U.S. Government Printing Office, May-June 1974).

[28] Quoted in *Watergate: Chronology of a Crisis*, Vol. II (1974), p. 200.

companies totaled $1 billion, about the same as Hartford's annual sales. Shortly after the settlement was reached in July 1971, McLaren left the Justice Department to become a federal judge, appointed by Nixon. He has denied being pressured by administration officials during the settlement negotiations.

The following year, columnist Jack Anderson wrote that Mitchell and ITT Washington lobbyist Dita Beard had arranged the out-of-court settlement in exchange for a promise that the company would contribute $400,000 to the 1972 Republican National Convention. Anderson's charges were based on a memorandum supposedly written by Beard to W. R. Merriam, ITT's Washington manager. The authenticity of the memo is still in dispute.

Outlook for Government Antitrust Action in 1975

Kauper, the antitrust division chief, said on Jan. 22 the Ford administration's recent shift in economic policy was no reason for relaxing antitrust standards. In a televised speech on Jan. 13 and in his 1975 State of the Union address to Congress two days later, Ford placed emphasis on pump-priming to fight a growing recession rather than on measures to choke off inflation.[29]

Kauper's division will continue to pursue a project to identify the extent to which government regulation stifles competition. Moreover, the Justice Department and FTC plan to make fuller use of economic analyses to determine how market power is concentrated. Questionnaires sent by the FTC in August 1974 to 345 of the nation's largest companies concerning profits, costs and related business activities have drawn refusals from some of the companies. Twelve of them have filed suit in federal district court in New York City seeking an injunction against the agency to block its information-gathering effort.

The new Antitrust Procedures and Penalties Act *(see p. 149)* is intended to eliminate behind-the-scenes political pressure on government antitrust officials. The new law requires the Justice Department to publish a "competitive impact" statement on every proposed consent decree, detailing the effect of the proposed settlement on prices and competition. In addition, the department is required to solicit public comment on the impact statement for a period of two months. The judge involved in approving the settlement must rule that the agreement is in the public interest.

And yet doubt remains that political pressures can be removed entirely from the antitrust process. Joseph C. Goulden,

---

[29] Kauper's remarks were in a speech to the Antitrust Section of the New York State Bar Association. For background on recent economic policy, see "Federal Fiscal Control," *E.R.R.*, 1975 Vol. I, pp. 23-40.

the author of a critical study of AT&T, *Monopoly* (1968), asked in
The Washington Post on Nov. 24, 1974, whether the new case
against AT&T will be "decided in United States District
Court, the statutory forum for cases brought under the Sherman
Antitrust Act, or in the figurative backrooms of Washington lobbying places where AT&T exercises power commensurate with
its rank as the nation's richest corporation." The answer to that
question, given the slow movement of antitrust cases, probably
lies several years in the future. In the meantime, the government vows that its antitrust effort will not be sidetracked.

Selected Bibliography

Books

Fusilier, H. Lee and Jerome C. Darnell, eds., *Competition and
Public Policy, Cases in Antitrust,* Prentice-Hall, 1971.
Goulden, Joseph C., *Monopoly,* G. P. Putnam's Sons, 1968.
Herling, John, *The Great Price Conspiracy,* Robert B. Luce, 1962.
Lekachman, Robert, *Inflation, The Permanent Problem of Boom
and Bust,* Vintage Books, 1973.
Morison, Samuel Eliot, Henry Steele Commager and William E.
Leuchtenburg, *The Growth of the American Republic,* Vol.
2, Oxford University Press, 1969.
Neale, A.D., *The Antitrust Laws of the U.S.A.,* Cambridge Uni-
versity Press, 1962.
Owen, Geoffrey, *Industry in the U.S.A.,* Penguin Books, 1966.
Tarbell, Ida M., *The History of the Standard Oil Company,* Peter
Smith, 1963 (originally published in 1904 by Macmillan).

Articles

"Bigness Under Attack: The U.S. vs. IBM," *Business Week,*
Nov. 11, 1972.
"Is John Sherman's Antitrust Obsolete?" *Business Week,* March
23, 1974.
"More For the Parts Than the Whole?" *Forbes,* Sept. 1, 1972.
Rogers, William, "IBM on Trial," *Harper's,* May 1974.
Smith, Richard Austin, "The Incredible Electrical Conspiracy,"
Fortune (in two parts), April and May 1961.
"Why the Justice Dept. Took AT&T to Court," *Business Week,*
Nov. 30, 1974.

Studies and Reports

Editorial Research Reports, "Business Concentration and Antitrust
Laws," 1966 Vol. I, p. 381.
Green, Mark J. with Beverly C. Moore Jr. and Bruce Wasserstein,
The Closed Enterprise System, Ralph Nader's Study Group
Report on Antitrust Enforcement, Grossman Publishers, 1972.
Green, Mark J., ed., *The Monopoly Makers,* Ralph Nader's
Study Group Report on Regulation and Competition, Grossman
Publishers, 1973.

REVENUE SHARING

by

Helen B. Shaffer

**1 9 7 5
Mar. 28**

REVENUE SHARING

S TATE AND LOCAL officials all over the country are
mounting a concerted drive to make revenue sharing a continuing feature of government. Under the general revenue sharing law of 1972, some $6 billion a year of federal tax collections
are being shunted, with relatively few strings attached, into the
coffers of 39,000 governmental jurisdictions in the nation.
Although the program is not due to expire until the end of 1976,
the governors, mayors and other local chieftains are clamoring
for assurance from Congress that the largesse will continue to
flow after that time. They speak of the need to plan now for the
future. Fiscal difficulties arising from the current economic
recession have added urgency to their pleas.

Congress is expected to begin consideration of the matter soon
after the White House makes good its promise to present the
lawmakers early in this session with a bill to extend revenue
sharing. President Ford, who as a member of the House of
Representatives had voted for the original act in 1972, has
reiterated his advocacy of revenue sharing on several occasions
since assuming the presidency. In his 1975 State of the Union
address on Jan. 15, and again in his budget message on Feb. 15,
he promised to send an extension bill to Congress in the near
future.

The bill is expected to follow the recommendations of a
revenue-sharing task force the President appointed in August
1974. After six months of study and consultation with state and
local officials and with leaders of interested private groups, the
task force recommended that the program be extended for five
years and nine months,[1] until Oct. 1, 1982. The task force also
suggested modest changes in the program. The most important
proposed reform is to increase the amount going to jurisdictions
of unusual need, typically big cities and communities suffering
severe joblessness.

Effective opposition to the principle of revenue sharing has
apparently declined since the debate that preceded the 1972

[1] The fractional-year recommendation is to accommodate the impending shift of the dates
of the federal fiscal year, which will run from Oct. 1 to Sept. 30 instead of July 1 to June 30,
beginning in fiscal year 1977.

enactment. Although many groups remain suspicious, by and large revenue sharing is regarded as one of the more benign legacies of the Nixon administration. President Nixon called revenue sharing the keystone of his plan for a "new federalism," but it does not bear a party stamp; there are supporters and opponents of revenue sharing on both sides of the aisle in Congress.

On the other hand, considerable criticism has been directed at the way the revenue-sharing program has been carried out and there is likely to be plenty of argument over terms of its renewal. Persons most critical of the program focus their complaints on the following claims: (1) that the distribution formula channels money to some communities that do not need it at the expense of those in dire need; (2) that too much is spent for projects desired by the affluent rather than the needy; (3) that racial and other forms of discrimination are practiced by some agencies receiving revenue-sharing funds; and (4) that the program provides insufficient opportunity for local citizens to participate in decisions on where and how the money is used. Because of such criticisms, advocates are running scared.

Issues of Debate Over Revision and Extension

Sen. Edmund Muskie (D Maine), a leading advocate of general revenue sharing, conducted four days of subcommittee hearings[2] in June 1974 to review operations of the program. He expressed concern that flaws in carrying out the purposes of the act had generated criticisms endangering the future of the program. "These criticisms are of particular importance," he said at the first hearing on June 4, "because revenue sharing was only reluctantly accepted by the Congress two years ago, and they portend at least some rough sledding when it comes up for renewal in the next Congress." He repeated the "rough sledding" prediction in a speech at a conference on American federalism,[3] Feb. 21, 1975. He said renewal "will be neither automatic nor easy."

Muskie favors making an effort to amend the law to meet some of the objections being raised by its critics; he believes this is the way to win more support for renewal. Other advocates—governors and mayors mainly—believe it is safer to keep modification proposals to a minimum. Thus they hope to avoid controversy and a splitting of the ranks of supporters. They prefer to concentrate on the need for keeping the plan going.

---

[2] Subcommittee on Intergovernmental Relations of the Senate Government Operations Committee. Muskie is the subcommittee chairman.

[3] Sponsored by the Advisory Commission on Intergovernmental Relations in Washington, D.C.

American Leaders on Revenue Sharing

"For a third of a century, power and responsibility have flowed toward Washington.... We intend to reverse the tide...."
Richard M. Nixon, television address, Aug. 8, 1969

"I believe strongly in general revenue sharing."
Gerald R. Ford Interview, June 15, 1974

"[Revenue sharing has been] a victim of the expansive rhetoric of the new federalism."
Edmund S. Muskie, Speech, Feb. 21, 1975

For a program that merely provides a mechanism for the transfer of funds from one governmental authority to another, revenue sharing has drawn an extraordinary amount of serious attention from governmental, citizens' and scholarly groups. "It is not an issue that generally stirs passions in its support," Muskie commented in his speech. Nevertheless, revenue sharing is recognized as a turning away from a long-growing trend in the federal system. This trend favored a proliferation of special grants from the federal to state and local governments, each accompanied by precise instructions on how and where the money was to be used. Under revenue sharing, money is simply handed over with minimal limitations on how it may be spent.

State and local officials have been delighted with this diversion from established categorical-aid procedure, which remains the dominant form of federal aid. They have praised the act as the rightful return of spending authority to officials closer to the will of the people, and hence better judges of how the money can be used for the benefit of the home community. Whether this is the way revenue sharing has actually worked out in its brief history is one of the many points of contention certain to arise in the coming debate.

Although the amount ($30.2 billion) to be shared over the five-year period (1972-1976) is not great relative to the total cost of running state and local governments,[4] the principle entailed is important. If general revenue sharing grows to become a major segment of the federal-aid system, it may presage fundamental shifts in the political relationships within the federal system. It may also alter the way tax funds are distributed for support of various public services and thus determine which segments of the population are likely to reap the most benefit.

Campaign by Governors and Mayors for Renewal

Major pressure for renewal comes from the leading organizations of state and local officials. These are the Council of State Governments, the National Governors' Conference, the National Legislative Conference, the National League of Cities, the U.S. Conference of Mayors, the International City Management Association, and the National Association of Counties. A coalition of these seven organizations, together with other state and local leaders, was formed in 1973 to iron out their differences on details so as to present a united front. Ideally, these leaders would like to have the revenue sharing made permanent, but they are willing to settle for a five-year extension. They are particularly concerned that renewal legislation be adopted no later than a full year before the existing authority for the program expires on Dec. 31, 1976.

The National Governors' Conference, at its meeting in Seattle in June 1974, adopted a resolution urging re-enactment of revenue sharing in 1975 in order to allow "adequate lead time for proper budget preparation." The National League of Cities, meeting in Houston in December, took the position that "long-term support of general revenue sharing is important to the continuance of effective local government in the United States." In a recent report the Advisory Commission on Intergovernmental Relations,[5] more than one-half of whose 23 members represent state and local governments, urged extension because "the program has strengthened our federal system." But it warned that revenue sharing was "a potential new source of intergovernmental tension."

The National League of Cities has appointed a special task force to keep watch on municipal interests in the conduct of the

[4] Revenue-sharing funds account for 1.3 to 2 per cent of an average state budget and possibly 5 to 10 per cent of local budgets, according to the Advisory Commission on Intergovernmental Relations. However, all forms of federal aid are calculated by the White House Office of Budget and Management to account for more than 20 per cent of state and local expenditures *(see table, p. 177)*.

[5] Advisory Commission on Intergovernmental Relations, *General Revenue Sharing: An* ACIR *Re-evaluation*, October 1974, pp. 1, 20. The commission was created by Congress in 1959 to monitor the operation of the federal system and to recommend improvements.

program and to guide strategy in the campaign to make the program a growing and permanent feature of the federal system. The task force, under the chairmanship of Mayors John Poelker of St. Louis and Moon Landrieu of New Orleans, undertook to win friends for revenue sharing among candidates for Congress in the fall of 1974. The task force is now directing the strategy for dealing with Congress during the months ahead. The league considers its activities in this area a success to date.

Effect on Financial Plight of States and Cities

The issue of revenue sharing returns to the political forefront at a time when the states and especially the major cities are facing serious financial problems. The combination of inflation and recession has had a devastating effect on their budgets. Only a year ago most of the states were in uncommonly good fiscal shape, with some showing surpluses. Today only a few are keeping ahead of their debts; the immediate prospect for nearly all of them is worse.

State and local treasuries recorded surpluses amounting to $19 billion in the last three months of 1972, the first quarter in which revenue-sharing payments were made, but only a $2 billion surplus at the end of 1974. Even that modest surplus was more apparent than real—it was due to a surplus in social insurance funds.[6] Operating funds for state and local governments hit a deficit of almost $10 billion by the end of 1974, as is shown in the following quarterly figures from the Department of Commerce:

1973 *(in billions)*				1974 *(in billions)*			
I	II	III	IV	I	II	III	IV
$4.5	$1.3	$-0.8	$-4.7	$-6.4	$-7.7	$-7.7	$-9.8

Figures exclude social insurance funds.

"The fiscal position of state and local governments worsened during 1974 because of stringent credit conditions and a slackened growth in receipts due to the slowdown in economic activity," the Federal Reserve Board reported.[7] The Joint Economic Committee of Congress forecast a $20 billion shortfall in the fourth quarter of 1974 "which could be expected to increase to as much as $25 billion...through 1975." It expected

---

[6] Even the social insurance surplus "was far from sufficient to meet the actuarial funding obligations imposed on pension plans for the employees of state and local governments."—Council of Economic Advisers, *Economic Report of the President*, transmitted to Congress, February 1975, p. 65.

[7] "The Economy in 1974," *Federal Reserve Bulletin*, January 1975, pp. 7-8.

that many state and local governments would have a hard time "to make it through the upcoming year without tax increases, employee layoffs, and cuts in levels of service.[8] However, the situation would vary among the states; those with deposits of natural resources would benefit from intensive development while those dependent on the manufacture of durable goods would suffer.

Events in early 1975 proved that those gloomy forebodings were well-founded. Some states were not only suffering operating-fund deficits but were running short of money to meet benefit obligations. Several states had to borrow from the federal government to meet unemployment compensation demands. New Jersey, which has suffered a general economic decline predating the present recession, had to borrow $150 million to meet its benefit obligations. Gov. Michael S. Dukakis of Massachusetts told a news conference on March 7 that his state was "dead broke" and facing an estimated $300 million budget deficit.

Inflation was playing hob with city budgets even before urban unemployment began to rise in 1974. Tax increases imposed in recent years were bringing in more revenue, according to a National League of Cities-National Conference of Mayors study, but this return still lagged far behind the increase in costs. The cities were worried about cutbacks in overall federal aid to states and local governments and a consequent decline in state aid to localities. "If state and local governments are to continue to carry out vital programs adequately...some provisions must be made to bridge the gap caused by inflation," the report stated.[9]

How bad the "urban fiscal crisis" had become was laid out on Jan. 31 before the Joint Economic Committee by Mayor Nicholas Panuzio of Bridgeport, Conn., speaking for the National League of Cities. A league survey, he said, showed that service budgets of more than 50 cities had increased by an average of 11.3 per cent in 1973 and 13.7 per cent in 1974. Increases in wages and fuel costs were major inflationary items.

Of 67 cities reporting, 36 were forced to postpone or cancel planned capital improvements and 42 would be compelled either to reduce services or raise taxes. Typical of capital improvement put aside because funds ran short were 150 public housing units (Gary, Ind.), rebuilding of old failing sewers (Santa Ana, Calif.),

---

[8] Joint Economic Committee of Congress, "Achieving Price Stability Through Economic Growth," Dec. 23, 1974, p. 65.

[9] National League of Cities-United States Conference of Mayors, *The Federal Budget and the Cities*, February 1975, p. 6.

bridge improvements (Cleveland), new fire station (DeKalb, Ill.), installation of street lights and purchase of police cars (South Bend, Ind.), and parks and recreation development (Norman, Okla.). Many cities were said to be in no position to provide "meaningful work" to their unemployed.

Growth and Varieties of Federal Aid

REVENUE SHARING represents a new development in the long unfolding history of federal aid to the states and localities. The fiscal relationship between the national and the state and local governments is a salient element of the American federal system. The changes that have taken place in this relationship over the years have done much to shape the political, economic and social structure of the nation.

In the beginning federalism was conceived as a duality: "two separate federal and state streams flowing in distinct but closely parallel channels."[10] This was taken to imply not only political autonomy within their separate domains but fiscal independence as well. The Constitution was mute on the question of federal aid. Presidents Madison in 1817 and Monroe in 1822 vetoed legislation to provide federal funds for "internal improvements." They said there was no constitutional authority for such funding. It was necessary, Monroe said in his veto message, to maintain "two separate and independent governments, one for local...the other for national purposes."[11]

Early Forms of Aid for Internal Improvements

President Jefferson in his second inaugural address in 1805 had proposed a constitutional amendment to permit use of federal funds for "internal improvements," education and other purposes. This proved to be unnecessary, however, for a pattern of intergovernmental cooperation was already developing. It involved a certain flow of federal bounty to the states and localities, though often by devious routes that obscured the true nature of the fiscal relationship. "From the initial session of the first Congress, a climate of intergovernmental cooperation in fiscal matters began to develop...."[12]

Perhaps the earliest form of federal aid was an act of Congress in 1790 providing that the federal government assume

---

[10] Jane Perry Clark, *The Rise of a New Federalism: Federal-State Cooperation in the United States* (1965, originally published in 1938), p. 9.

[11] Daniel J. Elazar, *The American Partnership in Intergovernmental Cooperation in the 19th Century* (1962), p. 16.

[12] *Ibid.*, p. 31.

the Revolutionary War debts incurred by the states. They received this aid in the form of federal bonds. Some historians trace the origin of federal grants to an act of Congress in 1803 that earmarked 5 per cent of the proceeds from the sale of federal lands for distribution to the states. The purpose was to help pay for roads and schools, but no legal requirements were imposed on use of the money.[13] Meanwhile, a surplus was building up in the U.S. Treasury from the proceeds of public land sales. To be rid of the unwanted surplus, Congress in 1836 provided that all but $5 million of it be given to the states in amounts relative to their representation in Congress. Some $28 million was paid out in three quarterly installments before the program was called off by the Panic of 1837.

Land Grants: Northwest Ordinances, Morrill Act

Over the years, the federal government gave away great tracts of land for internal developments with little effort to oversee state uses of the land or the money obtained from it. Land grants actually date from the pre-Constitutional period, when the Northwest Ordinances of 1785 and 1787 provided land grants to towns in the newly opened territories for the support of schools. This precedent was later extended to new states—beginning with the 17th state, Ohio, in 1803—as they were admitted into the Union. Not until near the end of the century when the open land began to run out did the land grant come to be supplanted by cash aid.

The most famous use of the land grant was provided by the first Morrill Act of 1862 which gave public lands to states for the establishment of colleges to teach the agricultural and mechanical arts as well as scientific, classical, and military subjects. The Morrill Act represented a new step in the unfolding of federal-state fiscal relations in regard to the "strings" attached to the grant: the federal government dictated the general nature of the subjects to be taught and required the land-grant colleges to submit annual reports on their finances and programs. This extension of the land-grant principle did not become law without opposition. Sen. James M. Mason (D Va.) in 1859 denounced the Morrill bill as "an unconstitutional robbing of the Treasury for the purpose of bribing the states."

"In the continuous forward surge of governmental services," writes a historian of American federalism, "the forms of federal-state cooperation constantly shift and merge with one another." Thus what began as a cooperative agreement eventually became a grant-in-aid "in which the federal government

---

[13] "A Brief History of Revenue Sharing," Appendix C of Brookings Institution study, *Monitoring Revenue Sharing* (1975).

Total Federal Aid to States and Localities

Fiscal year	Amounts (in billions)	Percentage of state-local expenditure	Fiscal year	Amounts (in billions)	Percentage of state-local expenditures
1960	$ 7.0	14.7	1973	$43.9	25.2
1965	10.9	15.4	1974	46.0	23.6
1970	23.9	19.1	1975 (est.)	52.6	23.3
1971	29.8	21.1	1976 (est.)	55.6	22.2
1972	35.9	23.0			

SOURCE: Office of Management and Budget.

makes payments to the states to help develop services which Congress has decided to aid."[14]

Several factors contributed to a growth of federal aid in the first quarter of the 20th century, a growth that lifted the annual total from $7 million in 1902 to $116 million in 1927. These were chiefly the emergence of major problems of national scope that required state or local as well as federal action, and the superior powers of the federal government to raise revenue, especially after the 16th Amendment to the Constitution was ratified in 1913, authorizing the tax on personal income.

The trend was toward enacting laws that gave federal funds for specific purposes, such as the Weeks Act of 1914 for agricultural extension activities, the Smith-Hawley Act of 1917 for vocational education, the Federal Highway Act of 1921, and the Sheppard-Towner Act of 1921 for maternal and infant health.[15] A Supreme Court decision in 1923 stilled criticism of the constitutionality of this form of aid; the Court held that the offer of grants did not violate sovereignty of the state because no state was required to accept the money and abide by the terms of the grant.[16]

Federal-aid funds multiplied during the Great Depression, leaping from $232 million in 1932, the last year of the Hoover administration, to more than $1 billion in 1934, the first full year of the New Deal. This funding receded somewhat in the following years but began a new upward climb after World War II. It continued to grow during the 1950s, despite President Eisenhower's often-avowed distaste for what he considered a trend toward socialism. The big era of federal aid growth, however, took place during the Kennedy-Johnson years; the total more than tripled in the 1960s. By 1974 it had reached $46.1

[14] Clark, op. cit., p. 137.

[15] This act was criticized so harshly as a government invasion of the private domain that, after one extension, it was allowed to expire in 1929, not to be revived until enactment of the Social Security Act in 1935.

[16] Massachusetts v. Mellon, Frothingham v. Mellon, 262 U.S. 447 (1923).

billion, representing an average annual growth since 1960 of 14 per cent.[17]

Meanwhile, the number of separate grant programs was proliferating, from an early base of only five in 1902. The Treasury Department's latest listing of federal grants to states and localities categorized them according to 90 separate federal government agencies that administer the programs. The actual number of grant programs is almost beyond count; the number is usually given as around 500 or more.

Events Leading to General Revenue Sharing Act

Support for revenue sharing grew in an atmosphere of mounting criticism of the abundance of federal grant programs by those who thought the time had come to simplify the whole aid system. The complaints heard most often were that (1) there were too many separate, uncoordinated and duplicating programs, (2) they required too much red tape to administer and placed too many restrictions on those who operated the programs, (3) they were too inflexible to respond to changing needs, and (4) there was too much remote control from Washington.

Adding to the critical atmosphere was the political discomfort of state and local elected officials who felt that the administrators and professional staffs of federally aided agencies were more responsive to the federal bureaucracy than to the political hierarchy of the states and localities. Governors complained two decades ago to the Commission on Intergovernmental Relations that some of their department heads were more loyal to the fund-dispensing agency in Washington than to them. The commission used the phrase "vertical functional autocracy" to apply to this political condition.

Early support for revenue sharing came from both major parties, but the reasons usually reflected the supporters' political bias. Conservatives tended to regard it as a substitute for categorical aid, while liberals tended to regard it as a supplement, especially in welfare and human rights fields. Rep. Melvin R. Laird (R Wis.) introduced a bill in 1958, for example, that called for a reduction of categorical aid in the amount of the proposed general revenue sharing fund. Six years later, Walter W. Heller, then chairman of the Council of Economic Advisers in the Johnson administration, proposed revenue sharing as a means of providing an outlet for expected surpluses in the federal budget.

---

[17] Office of Management and Budget, *Budget of the United States Government, Fiscal Year 1976, Special Analyses* (1975), p. 237.

In the same year, 1964, a task force on federal-state-local fiscal relations, appointed by President Johnson during his election campaign and directed by Joseph A. Pechman of Brookings Institution, was reported to have recommended a similar proposal. Johnson indicated in a statement on Oct. 28, 1964, that he liked the idea. The federal budget, he said, had a "comfortable margin" and should "help restore fiscal balance and strengthen state and local governments by making available for their use some part of our great and growing federal tax revenues over and above existing aids." However, he never followed through.

Pressure for revenue sharing continued to emanate from state officials and from Republicans in Congress. Fifty-seven members of Congress, 45 of them Republican, sponsored revenue-sharing bills in 1965-66. Both parties had revenue-sharing planks in 1968, but the Republicans gave theirs more emphasis.

Nixon first advocated a revenue-sharing plan in February 1968 when he was seeking the Republican presidential nomination. After his nomination, he appointed a task force on intergovernmental fiscal relations which reported to him on Nov. 29, soon after his election. The task force proposed that the federal government give one-half of one per cent of taxable personal income, about $1.75 billion, to the states. In April 1969 Nixon established an interagency committee on revenue sharing under the chairmanship of his economic counsellor, Arthur F. Burns, and then invited a representative group of governors, mayors and county officials to consult with the committee at the White House. He announced his first revenue-sharing proposal as President in a nationwide television address Aug. 8, 1969.

Five days later Nixon sent to Congress a message proposing legislation to turn back $500 million in fiscal year 1971 and more each year until the amount reached $5 billion in 1975. These figures were disappointingly small to many proponents. Congress took no action on the bill, although a subcommittee headed by Senator Muskie[18] held "information hearings" on revenue sharing in the fall of 1969. Muskie had meanwhile introduced a revenue-sharing bill at the request of the Advisory Commission on Intergovernmental Relations. In December 1970 the commission published an enthusiastic report under the title "Revenue Sharing—An Idea Whose Time Has Come."

Sharing Formula and Restrictions of 1972 Law

The next year, Nixon offered another revenue-sharing plan, bigger than the previous one, including both a bill for "general

---

[18] Subcommittee on Intergovernmental Relations of the Senate Government Operations Committee.

Allocation of Revenue-Sharing Funds

One-third of the money allocated to each state goes to the state government; the remainder is apportioned among local units of government. To determine how much each locality is to receive, each state is divided into geographic areas and an amount is earmarked for each area according to a formula that involves its population, tax effort and relative income. No area's share may exceed 145 per cent of the per capita entitlement for the entire state, and none may receive less than 20 per cent of the state's per capita entitlement.

Each area's allocation is then divided among its units of government also on a formula involving population, tax effort and income. The 145-20 per cent limitation is again applied, plus one other restriction: no unit may receive more than 50 per cent of its adjusted taxes and transfer funds.

The 145 per cent ceiling has been widely criticized. The Brookings study advocated its removal because it penalizes areas of low income or unusually high taxation. The President's task force on revenue sharing has recommended that the ceiling be lifted to 175 per cent of the average per capita payment to the state.

revenue sharing" and additional legislation for "special revenue sharing." "General revenue sharing" would provide money from the federal treasury to states and localities for them to spend more or less as they saw fit. "Special revenue sharing" would consolidate numerous existing categorical aid programs into six grants, each designated for spending in a broad area, such as education or manpower.

After extensive hearings, much debate and eventual compromise the general revenue sharing proposal became law under the name "State and Local Fiscal Assistance Act." President Nixon signed the measure on Oct. 20, 1972, in a special ceremony in Independence Hall in Philadelphia, at which he said he hoped revenue sharing would "renew the American federal system" that had been born in that city two centuries earlier. Of the special revenue-sharing proposals, only one became law. It was in the field of manpower, the Comprehensive Employment and Training Act of 1973. Since then, grants for community development and certain education programs have been consolidated. The term "special revenue sharing" is falling into disuse, supplanted by "block grants."

The State and Local Fiscal Assistance Act designated a five-year expenditure of $30.2 billion to be paid out in segments over seven designated "entitlement periods," beginning retroactively on Jan. 1, 1972, and terminating on Dec. 31, 1976. All states and nearly all general-purpose local governments were made eligible to receive a share of the fund. These comprised 50 state governments, the District of Columbia, 3,046 counties, 18,-778 cities, 16,986 townships, and 346 Indian tribes and Alaskan native villages. Each state's share was determined according to a complex formula based on population, urban population, per capita income, state income tax collections, and tax effort.[19]

The money received is not entirely "free"; a few restrictions are written into the law. Use of the money must meet requirements of state and local laws; it may not serve as matching funds to obtain other federal grants; and recipients must observe federal non-discrimination and labor standards. The law also establishes "priority expenditure categories" for use of the money by local governments for operating and maintenance costs. These categories are: *public safety* (police, courts, fire protection, etc.), *environmental protection* (water supply, pollution control, street cleaning, etc.), *public transportation* (highways, bridges, ice removal, etc.), *health, recreation, libraries, social services for the poor and aged*, and *financial administration.*

Problems for Future of Revenue Sharing

FROM THE START, revenue sharing has meant different things to different people. Not only have its advocates seen its merits in different lights but its critics have laid stress on different flaws and shortcomings. In the early 1960s, some economists saw it as a means of generating more spending for public services as an alternative to boosting the private sector through tax cuts. Nixon pushed it as a means of "returning power to the people" and de-emphasizing the "Great Society" grants of the Johnson administration. Governors and mayors saw it as rescue from their budget problems. Many others favored it because they viewed federal taxation, largely on corporation and personal income, to be more equitable than state and local taxes, which lean more on sales and property ownership.

Some were hostile to revenue sharing because they believed it would set back major social gains of the past few decades by

---

[19] Actually two formulas are used, one giving greater emphasis to the urban population factor. Whichever formula provides more money for the jurisdiction is the one accepted. If this results in either a shortage or a surplus of the total amount appropriated for all states in a particular entitlement period, then the deficit or the surplus is distributed proportionately among all recipients. The two-formula system was the result of a compromise between Senate and House versions of the bill.

Revenue Sharing Allocations, Through June 1975

Ala.	$ 345,757,045	Mont.	$ 80,707,069
Alaska	26,287,070	Neb.	146,153,449
Ariz.	204,004,530	Nev.	44,786,933
Ark.	211,748,980	N.H.	65,445,324
Calif.	2,174,444,621	N.J.	640,701,158
Colo.	214,225,230	N.M.	128,582,250
Conn.	258,962,785	N.Y.	2,275,641,249
Del.	61,250,628	N.C.	523,367,490
D.C.	91,015,007	N.D.	80,534,087
Fla.	596,657,019	Ohio	814,148,929
Ga.	426,376,912	Okla.	228,548,300
Hawaii	89,984,345	Ore.	202,571,585
Idaho	82,161,983	Pa.	1,072,440,757
Ill.	1,042,425,416	R.I.	91,778,114
Ind.	432,250,485	S.C.	279,707,246
Iowa	288,324,965	S.D.	90,248,250
Kan.	195,841,243	Tenn.	388,514,231
Ky.	332,853,707	Texas	966,721,718
La.	467,721,933	Utah	120,349,298
Maine	124,441,092	Vt.	57,415,982
Md.	403,879,235	Va.	404,672,683
Mass.	644,842,373	Wash.	294,357,431
Mich.	866,638,867	W.Va.	200,856,299
Minn.	404,924,014	Wis.	513,406,544
Miss.	334,567,815	Wyo.	37,676,954
Mo.	382,539,380	**Total**	$20,453,460,010

SOURCE: Office of Revenue Sharing

---

supplanting the categorical grants. Since the New Deal, organized labor and civil rights and human welfare activists have looked to the federal government as the effective righter of social wrongs to which many states and localities are indifferent or helpless to correct. As urban problems took on the dimensions of a major national problem, it was inevitable that reformist organizations would lobby for help in Washington rather than in 50 state capitals and thousands of financially strapped localities.

Labor Union's Fear of Setback in Social Gains

Organized labor opposed the Nixon administration on revenue sharing because it considered the plan a cover-up for an intent to reduce total federal aid. The Executive Council of the AFL-CIO warned in February 1971 that revenue sharing would "not add one penny to the money available to the states and localities." It would be "merely...a substitute for the full funding of existing programs" and "would block or slow down the needed expansion of grant-in-aid programs and the development of new ones." The Executive Council also complained that there was little assurance that recipient governments would abide by federal fair-labor and civil-rights standards.

A year after general revenue sharing got under way, the AFL-CIO indicated that its worst fears about the program and the motives of the Nixon administration in promoting it had been confirmed. The labor organization adopted a resolution in October 1973 calling for substantial increases in categorical grants of the traditional type and urging Congress to conduct oversight hearings on the operations of revenue sharing. "In the event that the abuses prove uncorrectible," the resolution stated, "[Congress should] abolish the program and re-direct the funds into appropriate categorical grants-in-aid programs." A few months earlier, a union economist had deplored the "let the states do it" approach of revenue sharing. "In the past the states were unable or unwilling to 'do it'," he wrote in the AFL-CIO newspaper, "and there is little reason to think the future will be any different."[20]

Critical Interest of Many Citizen Organizations

Few innovative government programs have undergone intensive monitoring and critical analysis from so many sources as this one. Aside from the multiplicity of government agencies that have been concerned with revenue sharing,[21] numerous citizens' organizations, civil rights groups and academic institutions have been giving revenue sharing close attention. The National Planning Association in December 1973 conducted a conference to review current studies and plan future research on revenue sharing and has put out four publications on the subject. The Brookings Institution, supported by a Ford Foundation grant, has been monitoring the program since its inception.

Four voluntary organizations, with financing from the Ford Foundation, established in the fall of 1973 a National Clearinghouse on Revenue Sharing, based in Washington, D.C. The four organizations—the League of Women Voters, the National Urban Coalition, the Center for Community Change and the Center for National Public Review—try to encourage more citizen participation in the decision-making process; they are also alert to civil-rights abuses and other alleged inequities. The Clearinghouse publishes a bimonthly newsletter and recently issued a report on a two-year study.

The Southern Regional Council in Atlanta began in mid-1973 to monitor the use of the revenue-sharing funds in 11 southern

---

[20] Arnold Cantor, "Revenue Sharing: The New States Rights," reprint from the *AFL-CIO American Federationist*, July 1973.

[21] Among the federal agencies that have monitored the program or given consideration to its operations in their reports are the Office of Revenue Sharing itself, the General Accounting Office, the Advisory Committee for Intergovernmental Relations, the Office of Management and Budget, the U.S. Commission on Civil Rights, the Equal Employment Opportunity Commission, the Civil Rights Division of the Justice Department, the National Science Foundation, Congressional Research Service of the Library of Congress, and several committees of Congress.

states, giving special attention to the effect on the minorities and the poor. The Center for National Policy Review in Washington, D.C., with a grant from the Rockefeller Brothers Fund, is studying the effects of the formula used for distributing the money. The American Friends Service Committee, in cooperation with the Women's Division of the United Methodist Church, has issued a comprehensive guide for monitoring the program by citizens' groups.

Complaint About Lax Civil Rights Protection

From these organizations have come bills of complaint. The Leadership Conference on Civil Rights, a coalition of 22 national voluntary organizations whose views had been solicited by President Ford's task force on revenue sharing, told him in a letter dated Jan. 20, 1975, that the task force recommendations "fail to deal adequately with serious problems implicit in the current revenue-sharing program." Investigations by "reputable academic, civil, community and religious organizations," the letter stated, "have brought to light serious deficiencies in how well the program serves the needs of minorities, women and the poor." The Leadership Conference said the task force recommendations would bring about only "cosmetic changes."

The U.S. Commission on Civil Rights has made similar complaints.[22] A typical complaint is that the money has gone to support a police or fire department that is biased in its hiring and promotion policies. In one case, blacks successfully pressed the charge that the money was used to pave streets only in sections where white residents lived. The most important case of this kind, for its effect on anti-discrimination enforcement, was brought against Chicago. The city was accused of failing to end discriminatory practices in its police department, which had received revenue-sharing money. A U.S. District Court in Washington, D.C., on Dec. 18, 1974, ordered the Treasury to withhold $19.2 million due the city for its next quarterly grant until the discriminatory situation was corrected.

Recipient governments are required by law to make periodic reports to the Office of Revenue Sharing on the uses to which revenue-sharing funds are put. These reports show that more than half of the money has been going to public safety, education and public transportation *(see table following page)*. Specific uses included an expenditure of $3.5 million by Salt Lake City for salaries of police personnel and fire fighters and $1 million by Norfolk, Va., to expand an art museum. ORS found little change in the distribution of general revenue-sharing ex-

---

[22] U.S. Commission on Civil Rights, *Making Civil Rights Sense Out of Revenue Sharing Dollars,* February 1975.

How Revenue-Sharing Funds Are Used

Usage	Per cent	Usage	Per cent
Public safety	23	Social services for poor and aged	4
Education	21	Financial administration	2
Public transportation	15	Libraries	1
Multi-purpose* and general government	10	Housing-community development	1
Health	7	Corrections	-1
Recreation	5	Economic development	-1
		Social development	-1

*Includes construction, renovation and maintenance of public buildings.
SOURCE: Office of Revenue Sharing

penditures over the short life of the program. Approximately one-third of the money has been going to capital investments, and two-thirds to operation and maintenance.

A number of studies, including ORS reports, point out, however, that the direct uses to which the money is put does not necessarily indicate the ultimate impact of the program. Summing up studies made by the General Accounting Office, Comptroller-General Elmer B. Staats pointed out the ease with which funds can be substituted in the governments' budgets.[23]

How well has revenue sharing been meeting its goals? The answer may depend on what the observer considers a major goal. That it has provided some relief, however small, to the recipient governments is implied by the eagerness of the state and local officials to hold on to the program. Some have complained that too much of the money has gone for capital expenditures rather than operating expenses—building a golf course, for example, instead of providing a welfare service to the needy. But capital expenditures can be defended both for the provision of a needed facility and as a job-creator in time of recession. Some objected that recipient governments used the money to hold down state and local taxes; others consider this a thoroughly valid use of the money.

Some friends of the program think too much has been expected of it. They say it should never have been intended to take the place of major categorical grants. Ideally, federal aid is viewed as a mix, with general revenue sharing taking its place with the others. Meanwhile, the present Congress can be expected to try to patch up the holes in the operation.

[23] Elmer B. Staats, "Intergovernmental Relations: A Fiscal Perspective," *The Annals* of the American Academy of Political and Social Science, November 1974, pp. 38-39.

Selected Bibliography

Books

Clark, Jane Perry, *The Rise of a New Federalism*, Columbia University Press, 1938.

Elazar, Daniel J., *The American Partnership in Intergovernmental Co-operation in the 19th Century*, University of Chicago, 1962.

Healy, Patrick III, *The Nation's Cities*, Harper & Row, 1974.

Nathan, Richard P., Allen D. Manvel, and Susannah E. Calkins, *Monitoring Revenue Sharing*, Brookings Institution, 1975.

Articles

Cantor, Arnold, "Revenue Sharing: The New States Rights," AFL-CIO *American Federationist*, July 1973.

Dales, Sophie R., "Federal Grants to State and Local Governments, Fiscal Year 1973," *Social Security Bulletin*, October 1974.

"The Crunch on City and State Budgets," *Business Week*, March 10, 1975.

"The Federal Government," *Federal Reserve Bulletin*, January 1975.

"The Future of General Revenue Sharing," *Nation's Cities* (journal of the National League of Cities), February 1975.

"How Fares Revenue Sharing?" *The Brookings Bulletin*, winter 1975.

Reports and Studies

Advisory Commission on Intergovernmental Relations, "General Revenue Sharing: An ACIR Re-Evaluation," October 1974.

—"Revenue Sharing—An Idea Whose Time Has Come," December 1970.

Editorial Research Reports, "Federal-State Revenue Sharing," 1964 Vol. II, p. 941; "Local Government Modernization," 1967 Vol. II, p. 737.

General Accounting Office, "Revenue Sharing: Its Use by and Impact on State Governments," August 1973.

Joint Economic Committee of Congress, "Achieving Price Stability Through Economic Growth," Dec. 23, 1974.

National Clearinghouse on Revenue Sharing, "General Revenue Sharing in American Cities: First Impressions," December 1974.

Office of Revenue Sharing, Department of the Treasury, "General Revenue Sharing—First Planned Use Report," 1973; "First Actual Use Reports," March 1974; "Second Annual Report," March 1, 1975; "What is General Revenue Sharing?" August 1973; "General Revenue Sharing: Reported Uses 1973-1974," February 1975.

Senate Government Operations Subcommittee on Intergovernmental Relations, hearings on revenue sharing, 2 vols., part 1 and Appendix, 1974.

U.S. Commission on Civil Rights, "Making Civil Rights Sense Out of Revenue Sharing Dollars," February 1975.

United States Conference of Mayors, "City Problems of 1975" (proceedings of convention, June 22-26, 1974).

INDEX

A